MEXICO: The Land, the Art and the People

PHOTOGRAPHS BY URSULA BERNATH

TEXT BY RICHARD GROSSMANN

MEXICO

THE LAND, THE ART AND THE PEOPLE

UNIVERSE BOOKS   NEW YORK

Translated and adapted by Marie-Christine Hellin

First American Edition
published in the United States of America in 1967
by UNIVERSE BOOKS, Inc.,
381 Park Avenue South, New York, N.Y. 10016
Library of Congress Catalog Card Number: 67–21 785
© Verlag Simon und Koch, Konstanz. All rights reserved.
No part of this book may be reproduced in any form without
permission in writing from the publisher, except by a reviewer who may
quote brief passages in a review to be printed in a magazine or newspaper.
Printed in Germany

TABLE OF CONTENTS

INTRODUCTION

Anyone who has not been to Mexico may have romantic notions about it. He may think of it as a country in the throes of continuous revolutionary ferment or see it as a lunar, volcanic landscape. It remains intangible; even intensive reading does not unlock the door to its riches and to its past. This book cannot therefore represent Mexico; it can only try to encourage the reader to explore Mexico on his own some day.

Mexico was settled by nomadic Indian tribes. These hunters had mongoloid features, although they were of different races. All of them came across the Bering Strait. The settling of the American continent took between 20,000 and 30,000 years. Some tribes settled in the region which is the Mexico of today, others went further south. In the Christian era, a number of Indian settlements in the highlands of Mexico developed into theocratic societies. The golden age of these small peoples produced achievements in the realms of architecture, sculpture and handicrafts which are comparable to those of contemporary European civilizations; a fact which is all the more astonishing since, as far as technology was concerned, they still lived in the Stone Age. This brief historical sketch of ancient Mexico will begin with the Archaic and the Olmec civilizations, i. e. the people from the rubber country.

According to the radio-carbon method, the oldest date established at La Venta on the southern Gulf coast is approximately 1150 B. C. The amazing Teotihuacán culture flourished in the first and second centuries A. D. Then came the Zapotecs, the Mixtecs, the Totonacs, the Toltecs and, above all, the Aztecs who built Tenochtitlán, their metropolis, on the very spot on which the capital rises today. We know them well because of the great heritage they left behind. They belonged to the Nahuas who, after migrating from the north of the continent, called themselves Mexica in honor of their greatest hero. The world-famous Maya civilization developed in the southern part of the country. The oldest date found on a stele in the Tikal sanctuary is 328 A.D.

The staple of the Mexican Indian was corn and it has been calculated that in order to grow their corn they only needed sixty or seventy days a year. As a result "leisure" civilizations developed. For some tribes, the cultivation of the soil led to the cultivation of the spirit. They were dynamic and endowed with great gifts, while other remained quite primitive. Why and where this quickening of the spirit occurred will always remain a mystery for us.

These magnificent civilizations were destroyed by the Spaniards. The Conquest began in 1519 with a handful of soldiers and a few cannons and was amazingly successful. Within a few years, the Spaniards acquired a territory inhabited by 10 million Indians whom they colonized, converted and enslaved. It is likely that by 1621 only two million Indians remained, so harsh was the treatment they suffered at the hands of their colonial masters. Undoubtedly they were also decimated by the plague. A new trend made itself felt: occidental civilization, Spanish art and the Christian mentality had a profound impact on the structure of Indian societies.

When Spain became embroiled in the Napoleonic wars, the *mestizos* threw off the Spanish yoke. The bloody uprisings lasted from 1811 to 1821. The independent Republic of Mexico was proclaimed in 1824. The mestizos became Mexicans from that day onward. It wasn't however until 1920 that the Mexicans won their freedom after costly wars against enemies inside and outside their country. Mexico then became the model of a successful revolution in Latin America.

Once they had achieved their independence, the Mexicans began to remember their glorious past. Archaeologists undertook the search for sanctuaries and religious centers of pre-Columbian days. More than 1500 sites were discovered; at present, excavations are proceeding in 48 of them. Untold riches still remain untapped. Historically speaking, both periods are essential: the pre-Columbian era of highly developed civilizations and the colonial age with its important churches and palaces.

The surface of Mexico covers 761,530 square miles. Of its more than forty-two million inhabitants, three and a half are Indians. The Government expends enormous sums to assist them. They will be integrated into the life of the nation in the not-too-distant future. The migration from the rural areas to the cities contributes to this process. Only 20 per cent of the land can be used for agriculture, while 43 per cent of the population lives in the rural areas. The majority work in industry in a few large cities, of which Mexico D.F. is the only one to have more than six million inhabitants.

Let us leave the cities to observe the life of the Indians who live in the far reaches of the provinces. They seem friendly and serene when they dance to the accompaniment of muted and dissonant instruments, when they drink *pulque*, when they watch their flocks of turkeys. However, in looking at the excavations and the jaguars, serpents and gods of destruction in the museums, we realize that even before their subjugation by the Spaniards with their forceful missionary activity, the Indians were governed by a caste of priests who filled their simple souls with demonic visions. The dark faces of the Indians whom we meet are often impenetrable and expressionless, as if they were reluctant to show their feelings and thoughts. Many of them are slightly stooped as if burdened by their past. They are not envious by nature and usually accept the inevitable without bitterness. The Indian is attached to his soil. When the Otomí Indians were transplanted by truck from the Mexqui valley, their arid home in the north, to a fertile southern province, they had just one reaction: quietly, they covered hundreds of miles on foot to return to their home valley. When they were questioned about their return, they replied that they "could not leave their dead all alone in the earth."

Mexico City, the hub of the country, is surrounded by volcanoes and high peaks and is situated in a valley which is 7800 ft. above sea level. It is the only city at that altitude with more than one million inhabitants on the whole continent. Its main arteries, the Avenida Insurgentes and the Paseo de la Reforma, are objects of national pride. A six-lane highway cuts through the most populated areas. Mexico City is spreading and building satellite cities, but the Government is seeking even greater decentralization. Every year, thousands of American tourists spend millions of dollars in Mexico. In 1964 alone, three new museums were opened in Mexico City: the National Museum of Anthropology, the Diego Rivera Museum and the Museum of Modern Art. There are four large universities with a student population of 130,000. On clear days, two snow-clad volcanoes tower above the city and the sky is crisply blue.

The Mexicans are proud of their land of the three thousand volcanoes. Sometimes the thin crust of their earth quakes and no one knows when and where a new volcano will appear next. The last one erupted during the Second World War in the State of Michoacán. Mexican moods tend to vary frequently, so does the landscape. There are times however when it seems as if all the shouting and singing could not pierce the great silence which covers prehistory. Somehow the Mexican lives from day to day. He is Catholic; his faith accepts the realities of the flesh and thus becomes more profound. He combines Spanish and Indian traits: he possesses some quixotic qualities, namely a tremendous imagination as well as terrible self-doubts. He likes to pretend that nothing can impress him. Kindheartedness hides beneath his dreams of glory, quick perception beneath his self-seeking. His naiveté and family spirit are very endearing and his hospitality is boundless. He tries not to get caught up in the financial arrangements of others. Ancient Indian insights underlie his sadness. He has thrown off many burdens and is a free man now. His music is melodic, not harmonic, and is at its best when it is melodramatic. The Mexicans are a youthful nation.

TEOTIHUACÁN

A new highway leads to the ruins situated some thirty miles north of Mexico City. To our right, on the high plateau, flocks of patient sheep graze. The two largest pyramids are visible from afar. Blue mountains on the horizon complete the stage-set. They are outlined in red while the whole valley is bathed in the golden morning light. We stop. Flights of vultures circle above us in the hot dry air and the cicadas loudly sustain one single high-pitched note.

We enter the sanctuary zone. The people who are climbing the Pyramid of the Sun look like ants. The pyramid dominates the entire zone; it rises to a height of 216 ft. and is 761 by 721 ft. at the base. It is truncated at the top so as to provide a magnificent base for altars and temples. The few graves in the socle were probably used for the burial of construction victims. The Pyramid of the Moon is 150 ft. high and 426 by 511 ft. at the base. That the religious motivation of the Teotihuacáns must have been very strong is demonstrated by the massive materials they managed to move to the sanctuary zone without the help of machines. Archaeologists have probed deep into the pyramids and have established that they were built simultaneously.

Excavation has been going on for approximately forty years. It is supposed that a city with temples, monasteries and residential sections flourished here from 200 B.C. to 600 A.D. It has been estimated that it may have had some 150,000 inhabitants. Not even their name is known to us. In the 14th century, the Aztecs gave the name of Teotihuacán to the destroyed temple district. The meaning of the word is "place where one becomes god-like." The Aztecs believed that, after death, kings become gods. The largest pyramids were named for the sun and the moon because, according to Aztec mythology, the sun and the moon were the result of the self-immolation of two gods. No one knows the reasons for the complete extinction of this sanctuary.

In 1370, when the Aztecs founded Tenochtitlán, the city on the lagoons which is the capital today, Teotihuacán had already lain in ruins for more than 500 years.

There is an overwhelming feeling of loneliness here. Small white clouds float over the sky towards the Gulf. A brooding silence lies over the 1860 acres which were once densely populated. Here and there one sees the dusty green of the maguey and many "pirul" trees with trembling leaves. One is struck by a court in the central part of the site which the Spaniards called *ciudadela*. From the south side of the Pyramid of the Moon, the Highway of the Dead runs straight as an arrow, past the Pyramid of the Sun, to the *ciudadela*. Perhaps the Aztecs gave it that name because they thought that the mounds on both sides of the Highway were tumuli; however, the archaeologists have only found them to be temple hillocks, not burial places.

We rest in the wild grass beneath a "pirul" tree and enjoy the fragrant breeze.

Later on we visit Tepantitla, half a mile east of the Pyramid of the Sun. In 1942, a farmer found walls with frescoes while tilling the soil. Careful cleaning revealed multicolored representations of the water god. The most precious find, however, was the wall of a house representing this lost people's view of paradise: human beings dancing among butterflies, blooming cacao trees and merry rivers. The domain of Tlaloc, the rain god, in the midst of the dry high plateau is also depicted. On other frescoes one sees hands holding tigers. Just as in Pompeii, one finds that occasionally children of a thousand years ago scratched a game somewhat like ticktacktoe into the frescoes, undoubtedly to the annoyance of their parents. Clay figures, sculptures and frescoes indicate tremendous artistic riches. Colorful birds, butterflies, tigers, parrots, shells and snails are fascinating both because of their realism and their symbolic content.

Clay figures from Teotihuacán which could be dated were found in the south in the Maya excavation sites. Archeologists think that, for centuries, Teotihuacán was a place of pilgrimage and barter for all of northern central America. It may have been destroyed by warring tribes from the north. Much remains a mystery; it is unlikely that we will ever know how the Teotihuacáns attempted to resist destiny.

Slowly we return to the *ciudadela*. The west side of the pyramid situated in its inner court yard is world-renowned. Luckily another pyramid had been built in front of it so that it was found fully preserved beneath the stones and soil which had covered it. It is decorated with a striking relief: serpents coil around sea shells, their plumed heads protrude threateningly from the wall; Quetzal-cóatl, the plumed serpent, alternates on the façade with the head of Tlaloc, the rain god.

There is a feeling of great violence in these ferocious works of art created in an age which also excelled in masks of the utmost nobility. Perhaps the reason for this is that many different forces are at work in primitive peoples. There must have been violent religious tensions in the Teotihuacán culture which finally either led to its downfall or at least prepared the way for it. The sanctuaries give the visitor the impression of listening to a tale full of suspense and melancholy.

PALENQUE, CITY IN THE JUNGLE

A small airplane takes us from Villahermosa to Palenque in exactly forty-four minutes. We land on a smooth airstrip in the midst of fields and clamber into an ancient taxi which bounces towards Palenque along a road which is really the dried-out bed of a brook. Man-sized weeds grow in the empty wilderness on both sides. Gradually our path takes us into the trees and we can no longer see beyond the green walls. Swamp smells mingle with the scent of flowers and of the earth on the mountain sides.

We have barely shut our eyes when we reach our destination. Hills crowned by temples rise in the midst of the jungle. They look like gray, moss-covered ships lying at anchor for all time.

The loneliness of the site would be oppressive, were it not for the songs of many birds. Light and shadow move over the site and the tree tops of the forest.

Just in front of us is the pyramid on which the whole palace was built; a high tower rises above it. From the top we have a view of the eerie ruins and their surroundings.

The Maya ruins are situated in the heart of the rain forest of the Usamacinta river in the State of Chiapas. We don't even know their real name. Palenque, meaning "the site of the palisades," was the name given to them by the Spaniards. Hieroglyphics which have been deciphered indicate that this temple district flourished in the 7th century A.D. The site was deserted in the 9th century for unknown reasons and the forest grew over it and buried it for eight centuries. In the 16th century, the Spaniards discovered it and in 1839 John Lloyd Stephens, an American diplomat and amateur archaeologist, happened upon the ruins and described them enthusiastically. Catherwood, his traveling companion, sketched and painted them, adding to his sketches restorations of what he imagined to have been there.

Below us, three Indians mow the tall wild grass with their long machetes. A tired, dun-colored horse looks on. The Otulun brook cuts through the site. Beyond it, there are three hills. A temple rises on each of them: the *Templo del Sol,* the *Templo de la Cruz* and the *Templo de la Cruz Foliada.* The palace lies at the foot of the tower. Almost directly across from it stands the *Templo de las Inscripciones,* the highest of the temples. To the north, one sees the *Templo del Conde* and the *Templos del Norte.* A steep mountain covered with vegetation rises beyond the southern group of temples. The wind carries a sweet scent towards us. We can see very far into the strange landscape below us.

Then we climb one hill after another, visit the temples and rest on their steps.

Four inner courts surrounded by loggias add to the vast dimensions of the palace ruins. The tower undoubtedly served as an observatory from which the priest-astronomers watched the celestial bodies and their laws night after night. The numerous reliefs carved from stucco and limestone are a delight not necessarily lessened by the fact that moss has grown over them and that wind, sun and rain have damaged them. In fact, just because of these inroads of time they have taken on a new charm. The colors are fascinating. Mosses and tiny furry plants live in the low reliefs and color their outlines. They have penetrated elbow and knee joints, tunic folds and eyes, and have shaded, colored and blurred their outlines. In spite of these magic changes, plumes vibrate on heads. Lordly elegance, nobility of mien, expressive gestures and serene glances remain. Where the Maya sculptors have used stucco, a softer and more brittle material, the texture of the slabs is reminiscent of that of human flesh.

Block after block in the inner chambers is covered with orange, pink and peacock-blue loops. Dark brown and sea green alternate with dark gray and olive green. Small trees and bushes growing out of cracks also cast their greenish light over the sculpted fragments. Their roots force their way up through the stones and spread all over the sacred chambers.

The great number of temples rising on the densely overgrown hills shows that Palenque was governed by priests. The chambers may well have been dedicated to the gods but the servants were the real rulers. A Mexican archaeologist, Alberto Ruz Lhullier, discovered a tomb in 1952 which seems to prove this view. It is a huge monument beneath the *Templo de las Inscripciones*. Steep, damp steps go down some 98 ft. into the heart of the sacred mountain. The Maya arch was used in the construction of the vaulted burial chamber. It is decorated with offerings and the huge slab on the sarcophagus is sculpted in the classical style. Ruz found jade jewelry and a giant pearl. The skeleton was painted red; it wore a pectoral and rings on every finger. The manner in which the tomb is built shows that the priests were as circumspect as statesmen. The stairs leading to it were sealed off completely with stones.

It is to be surmised that the life the Mayas led near these temple hills was dominated by religion whether they dragged heavy blocks to construction sites, planted corn or chiselled sculptures out of stones.

All the buildings must have been covered with multicolored paintings. Filigreed, crest-like structures on the roofs of the *Templo de la Cruz* and the *Templo del Sol* bear witness to the simplicity and refinement of Maya architecture. The beautiful high reliefs inside the *Templo de la Cruz Foliada* and the *Templo del Sol* do not show any trace of the wistfulness of later Maya cultures; they express youthful vigor.

We climb to the top of the observatory once more. It is difficult to convey the atmosphere of these ruins. The jungle crowds them from every direction. Two enormous butterflies, lemon-colored and dotted with black, flutter about us for a long time. The Government would have to expend millions for the preservation of these grandiose ruins and therefore it is likely that the temples will return once more to the jungle which had swallowed them up centuries ago. The song of the cicadas grows louder. Others answer on a higher note and then suddenly fall silent. We are between day and night, dusk is extinguished when a dark-blue shield covers the sky and the first three stars begin to sparkle.

MAYA RUINS IN UXMAL

As far as the eye can see there is no end to the plain. We set out from Mérida to visit the Maya ruins in Uxmal. Here and there the soil tries to resist the invasion of the underbrush. Vultures circle above us in giant loops. Nothing else moves, nothing troubles a landscape where wilderness borders on carefully cultivated land.

On both sides of the road there are endless sisal (henequen) plantations. They look like the maguey, the agave from which pulque is distilled, but these are the *agavas rigidas,* a type of maguey which provides the fibrous raw material for one of Yucatán's most important industries.

The rows run parallel to each other and the distance from one plant to the next has been measured down to the last inch. The henequen provides one of the cheapest hard fibers in the world and, even today, still constitutes the wealth of the Yucatán peninsula. The fluctuations of its prices on the world market keep the area in a state of constant agitation.

The white-washed haciendas of the plantation owners can be seen between the rows of supple, grayish-green plants. Sometimes the light shines on one of their pointed leaves in such a way that it looks as if the maguey were on fire.

We reach our destination after a short, 48-mile drive. The ruins lie before our eyes, abandoned, lonely, half obliterated and majestic. First we climb the steep stairs of the pyramid which is called the House of the Magician. Many additions were made to it. Five times temples were erected on the various terraces from which the pyramid slowly grew. Chac, the rain god, is represented on the decorated façades and the head of a priest protrudes from the jaws of a stone serpent. The origin of the edifice is not known. The legend which explains the name of "Magician" is as follows: A witch bore a child in an egg. There was much ado about the witch's child. The king of Uxmal demanded that the child prove its magic origin and commanded it to build a palace in a single night. The witch helped the child and the palace was finished in the morning. The king then demanded that the child break coconuts on its own head. The witch put a magic disc on the child's head and the coconuts broke on it. As a result the king had to relinquish his power and the child became the king of Uxmal. This legend resembles fairy tales from all over the world which also hinge on a riddle that must be solved.

From up here we can see all about us ruins and hills overgrown with grass which still await excavation, a grand design with large spaces for gatherings reserved between the sanctuaries.

The Nunnery stands in an immense quadrangle not far from the House of the Magician. The Spaniards probably chose that name because of the many cells built into it. A temple in the court bears the name of the planet Venus. Stairs ascend, masks of Chac decorate the walls. We see sculptures with turtle bodies and the heads of old men. Two giant stone serpents cross each other on the wall as they creep along. The rattles on their tails are decorated with plumes. Reliefs representing tatooed warriors "spring" from the wall. A mysterious world of symbols.

The four nunnery palaces differ in size and face in different directions. Everything has been restored with care. The Mayas had considerable artistic sensibility, a vigorous and simple talent for sculpture and used geometrical precision in expressing it. This was undoubtedly due to the influence of the Toltecs from the north.

We cross a vast, airy terrain to the House of the Governor, where a long center building, extended further by two wings, stands on a 588 ft. long terrace. Stone ornaments form garlands. The Quetzalcóatl labyrinthine motif is repeated with harmonious regularity. The relationship between the proportions has been studied down to the last detail. The edifice is massive and yet airy – open to the world – lucid in conception. The water gods on which rain and, therefore, fertility depend play a dominant role in Maya theology. That is why, not far from here, on the House of the Turtles – one finds a frieze of stone turtles used as water symbols. In the Temple of the Pigeons one is fascinated by ornaments resembling church gables. The cornice of the building is decorated with a high relief, but the archaeologists still do not know its meaning. The plastic art in Uxmal has acquired the patina which bodies hewn from stone sometimes possess.

We sit down, somewhat stunned, on a carved stone block near an exciting stone sculpture which stands in front of the House of the Governor and try to understand what has happened to us. Next to us a Maya sculptor has forced two jaguars into each other so that their backs form a throne while their heads which are turned away from each other form the armrests of this lordly couch. The Mayas must have been a strong nation and their priests very spiritual; they lived both modestly and undauntedly under their laws. Thousands of questions beset us: From where did the Mayas come? When? What were they seeking, what did they find?

Some facts are known about them, but not the decisive ones. We know that, suddenly, about 300 A.D., a highly developed Maya civilization suddenly blossomed whose origin and development remain completely unexplained to this day. A similar phenomenon occurred at the same time in Monte Albán and in Teotihuacán. At that time the Mayas lived south of the Mexico of today in the highlands of Guatemala, in El Salvador and in Honduras and therefore in moist, boundless jungles. It is difficult to grasp that the Mayas actually lived in the stone age since they lacked the wheel, metal tools, animals to carry their burdens and the potter's wheel. We are touched by their mastery of sculpture and their imposing architecture. We know that priests and farmers lived together in harmony in peaceful city states. No weapons have been found. The population cultivated its fields, participated in the numerous religious holidays and attended the temple ceremonies on the pyramids built with its arduous labor – it may well have failed to understand the intellectual pursuits of its priests. It had full confidence however in their astrological knowledge. The Maya intelligentsia was fascinated by the continuous flight of time, by the idea of the eternal past and of the future which is eternally closing in on us. The Maya priests surpassed all contemporary astronomers in the knowledge of this science. They studied mathematics and astronomy without the help of instruments and minutely observed the course of the sun and the stars for centuries. They arrived at the concept of the "zero" by a remarkable intellectual process and in this achievement as well they were superior in their time to all the mathematicians in other parts of the world. By calculations similar to those of the Jews and the Romans they arrived at the conclusion that their history began in the year 3113 B.C.

But at present we are in Uxmal – a long way from Guatemala. How is it that there are Maya ruins all around us? It remains a puzzle to this day why – in the 9th century A.D. – the Mayas suddenly moved to Yucatán. They completely abandoned their great temples, although it had taken them centuries to build them, and founded new sanctuaries in Yucatán; Uxmal was one of them. Archaeologists have various theories about this unique migration, but until now no one has discovered its true cause. Slowly, we walk through the ruins once more. Uxmal has come full circle: it has served life and has now sunk back into nature.

VIRGIN FOREST IN QUINTANA ROO

Tree ferns and mullein grow on the edge of the forest. A vulture circles slowly in the burning light above the trees. Coconut palms tower above the mangrove thicket. Everywhere swamp plants encroach on twisted tree trunks. Creepers form an impenetrable bottle-green jungle. Inside the forest, it is night; only here and there does the light pierce the dense foliage. Black bogs bubble and shadows

16

move. Flamingo-red blossoms cover a bush. **Delicately** colored convulvulus clambers wildly over branches. Lianas are strung from tree to tree like garlands. Everywhere dark balls of parasitic growth have fastened onto the tangle. Orchids show their serpent's tongue. Chaos, anarchy – life and death intermingle.

There are feverishly convoluted branches and stone-hard mahogany trunks. Swamp cypresses violently force their way upwards. Aerial roots hang down like snakes. Deep in the forest parrots and monkeys take turns in outscreeching each other. Bright-yellow and tar-black blossoms flower. The virgin forest creaks, drips, luxuriates and blooms because it is dying.

MONTE ALBÁN

We could hardly tear ourselves away from the jewels exhibited in glass cases in the Museum of the City of Oaxaca, from the necklaces, earrings and bracelets made of gold, jadeite, agates, turquoises, rock crystal, onyx, jaguar bones, silver and alabaster. On the 9th of January 1931, Caso, a Mexican archaeologist, discovered these riches in a tomb on top of a mountain which rises above Oaxaca named Monte Albán by the Spaniards. It is the most precious archaeological find ever made in Central America.

We walk up the wide loops of the road leading up the mountain. The scent of flowers is heady; a machete is being sharpened somewhere, cries from a farmyard where Indian children play with excited turkeys pursue us. Below us we see Oaxaca, once the capital of the Zapotec Indians. We watched the men this morning when we sat in the *zócalo*, the market place, and listened to their melodious speech. Their ancestors lived here for many centuries and their sanctuary stood on the top of the mountain. The higher we climb, the more we see of the three fertile valleys below. The air is mild, almost tropical.

To our surprise, when we reach the top we find a vast flat terrain rather than a peak. It looks as if it had been levelled and fashioned by industrious hands. There are ruins as far as the eye can see. Nothing could be more pleasant than to lean against a large rock in this honey-colored noonday light, to follow the birds and the small feathery clouds with our eyes and to evoke the past.

The archaeologists did not encounter any water during their excavations, nor did they find any weapons. It is believed that the mountain served exclusively as a temple site and not as a fortress. Whatever the direction in which one turns, one sees valleys furrowed by roads down below. It was a brilliant strategic choice for a sanctuary site. In the distance we see the silver-blue outline of mountains against the horizon. The sacred buildings lie before us cloaked in light and silence. A series of buildings stands in the middle of the terrain which is rectangular in shape and surrounded by pyramids on all sides. One is struck by one of the pyramids which is not in line with the rest and looks almost as if it had turned away. It is believed that, for centuries, the Zapotec priests observed the sun and the stars from it with fanatic thoroughness. Their astrology grew out of their knowledge of astronomy and they used it boldly to predict the future. Theirs was a theocracy; in other words, the gods reigned supreme and every aspect of life was governed by religion. An account given in a preserved chronicle tells of a priest-duke who lived ascetically, could not be approached by his people and took all the decisions for them.

We walk up and down among the sacred buildings. The rectangular terrain is about 2275 ft. long. Time and again the unfinished, or rather truncated, pyramids are crowned by the remnants of temples. Sometimes only one flight of stairs leads to the top, sometimes there are four such flights, one on each side. There is a ball court which also had a religious purpose. The temple façades have indented double cornices typical of Zapotec architecture. One of the steles on the south platform represents in relief prisoners with their hands tied behind their backs. The more we walk about, the more we become aware of the fact that these sacred buildings are integral parts of a grand design which, in turn, relates to the surrounding landscape. The boldness of its conception is not even surpassed by the designs of the Egyptians.

The Zapotec civilization is considered to have been one of the most amazing in Mexico. Its golden age lasted about 400 to 800 A.D.; moreover, particularly deep excavations led to finds from five different cultural eras. Time destroys or preserves the monuments of history according to its own strange whims. Zapotec architects certainly loved to build stairs. An amazing flight of stairs on a pyramid on the north side of the site is 140 ft. wide. It may have been meant to symbolize the hierarchical laws. All the steps in Monte Albán are very high so that the ritual ascents and descents were slowed down to a ceremonial pace by natural means. Next to a temple situated on the western part of the plateau, we suddenly come upon strange reliefs carved on stone slabs. The limbs of the religious figures are strangely twisted and glyphs pour from their mouths. It is said – and tradition is often right – that they are *danzantes* – dancers. Their faces could be Olmec faces and could hail from the Gulf culture which seems to have been the cradle of almost all the Mexican art forms.

We are at an altitude of almost 6175 ft. A pleasant mountain wind brings us the scent of flowers and grass. Two shaggy donkeys' heads appear from a sunken farmyard, stare at us for a long time, shake themselves almost simultaneously and resume their grazing. Ghostlike and pleasant.

Caso succeeded in finding more than one hundred and fifty tombs, among them religious tombs with antechambers and main chambers. In some of them the blocks at the entrance were decorated with reliefs and the stucco-covered inner walls were brightly painted. Zapotec clay vessels were found in the tombs into which patterns had been scratched before they were fired. They showed realistic human faces. Some represented Cócijo, the rain god, with a cleft serpent's tongue. Censers were found in the tomb which had been broken deliberately so as to free their "soul" for service to the dead. A big urn made of black clay stands in a niche in the façade of tomb No. 104. It represents the corn god. His great headpiece is made of the plumes of a rare and revered bird, the quetzal; his nose and ears are weighed down with jewelry; he holds a sceptre and a small mask hangs on his chest. The Mayas also wore pectoral masks and this shows the ties which existed with Teotihuacán, the other cultural metropolis of that time. A large clay figure was found in one of the tombs of this great necropolis. It represents Xipe-totec, "our skinned master," as he was called by the Zapotecs to convey the double meaning of self-sacrifice and sacrifice of a stranger, because this god always put on the skin of a flayed victim to symbolize the renewal of nature in the spring. The dead were accompanied to the grave by the most choice and beautiful objects. One gains the impression of an attempt, born of fear, to placate the gods and to facilitate the "life" after death of the dead. One wonders why the Zapotecs always felt that the gods were threatening and angry.

In the 14th and 15th centuries, the Mixtecs pushed south and drove the Zapotecs from their holy mountain. They immediately proceeded to use the tombs for their own dead. The world-famous tomb No. 7 became the burial place of a Mixtec nobleman who was given the fantastic jewelry which we admired this morning in the Oaxaca museum. The conquerors used – not iron and steel – but stone tools with amazing mastery to fashion many materials into jewels of which we would be proud today.

But enough about the tombs and their symbols. We climb the stairs of the next pyramid because we feel that softness in the air which enhances the evening light in Mexico. The mountains to the east which look like a storm cloud have turned completely red. The mountains in front of them have taken on an incredible purple hue above the pink dusk. To the west, the outline of the mountain ranges behind which the sun is setting slowly emerges from the silver haze of the foot hills. At first they seem but a dream, but at last they stand out clearly in the vanishing light. The stone blocks of the observatory have taken on an unearthly light, as if they were made of glass and illuminated from within. Now the first lights sparkle in the valleys and the song of innumerable cicadas begins.

MARKET DAY IN TLACOLULA

From a distance one already hears the undefinable sounds; many voices, but the language cannot possibly be Spanish. The market is held right next to the church square. No end of huts and stands overflowing with goods, but most of the Indian women sit on the ground, their legs tucked under them and spread their wares out in front of them.

Indian men, all of them wearing sombreros, crowd in a double circle around a hawker. They cannot take their big dark eyes off his. The man's hands reach for a glass. Small white pellets roll about in it. He raises the glass high above his head. Immediately all eyes follow it upwards. With the other hand he reaches for a small piece of paper. All the dark eyes hasten to look at the paper. He begins to question them loudly: "What do your children need?" Silence. "Vitamins is what they need. Without vitamins they will remain small and puny. What do you need? Vitamins to build your blood. If your children don't have good blood, they won't grow strong and able to help you. You need them to help you raise your corn. I mean well; I am not forcing you to buy, but I'll make each of you a present of a vitamin tablet. Give them to your children and they will grow strong. Here you are!"

He wraps white pellets in small sheets of gray paper and immediately all the hands reach out for them. He gives one to every person present. No one thanks him; they look silently at their gifts. Then someone on the outside of the circle calls out: "Give me a box of vitamins!" And suddenly two, three, seven of them buy.

The others disperse. The vitamin hawker squats on the ground next to his boxes, exhausted and grinning, and slowly chews a vitamin tablet.

Suddenly we hear pigs squealing and the bleating of sheep. They are tied to a post, while next to them some very serious-looking Indians bargain. All of them are Zapotecs and speak their own language among themselves. To us it is no more than a strange buzzing and hissing. All of them are coffee or earthcolored. Their hair is dark and shiny, their teeth to be envied. Under the noonday sun, the women wear their gray rebozos wrapped around their heads like turbans.

There is no end to the wealth of goods offered. Over here you find dried fish and crabs from the Gulf, over there familiar fruit: bananas, apples, oranges, lemons, coconuts and avocados. Next to them lie the stranger varieties: the mango, with its indescribable, refreshing aroma; cobalt-blue and turquoise-green figs; orange pomegranates whose coarse-grained flesh tastes of gooseberries; perfumed, head-sized papayas, reddish-yellow and juicy; mountains of pineapples; the tasty, brown mammey – a heavenly scent emanates from hundreds of fruits and flowers.

Home-made tortillas are offered for sale everywhere. Black, green and red chilis are much in

20

evidence. There are stands full of cheap, violently bright clothes, many of them orange and electric green. Next to them lie shoes and sandals. Indian men sell shiny hemp ropes, light-colored baskets and harnesses. Frightened turkeys and chickens lie on the ground, their feet tightly tied together.

An enormous square. Everyone pushes, crowds and calls. Dogs bark and chase one another. Some women sit on the ground, minding three or four offspring. On a piece of old newspaper in front of them they have carefully piled up five onions and four tomatoes. That is all they have to offer and they wait for a buyer hour after hour. Parrots and parakeets shriek. Colorful, cheap jewelry is praised with hoarse voices. The antiquated loud-speakers of the vendors are deafening. Tightly braided straw mats have been put down on the ground. In their huts, the Indians use them as beds. Here, silent women kneel on them behind their wares, just looking. They seem to look right through us, as if we did not exist. Their faces are expressionless and indolent. Many of them come a great distance, their children on their backs and they must go back in the evening. The color contrasts are violent and strange and yet they harmonize somehow. Tastefully arranged flower bouquets lie on the ground awaiting buyers. People meet and exchange goods and news like a big family at a get-together. Underfoot, small boys chase each other. The smells are overwhelming. Babies are nursed publicly. The people eat pork which has just been roasted, immediately, without even sitting down. The sweet scent of lilies mixes with the smell of onions. The lilies win out.

Now we come across a section of the market in which the ground is covered with brown and bottle-green glazed pottery. An Indian kneels behind black clay vessels which fascinate us by their realism: dogs, ducks, sirens and vases. These small figures bring to mind the perfection of the distant past. We ask the Indian: "Where does this pottery come from?" He replies in halting Spanish: "From S. Bartolo Coyotepec." "Where is that?" "A few miles from here." His expression is both impassive and speculative. "How much is this dog?" His whole face begins to work, even his mouth opens and closes silently. Long moments later, he comes up with the price: "Ten pesos." "Much too expensive." He leaps up, pushes back his sombrero, quickly picks up the dog and a siren, holds both of them out to us and says "Together they will be twelve pesos." A young Indian who has been squatting on the ground behind his pile of brown pottery, comes over filled with curiosity. "Too expensive, much too expensive." We walk on and look at many other displays, but there is nothing we like quite as much as the black dog. We turn back slowly and are still 15 ft. from the dog, when his owner calls out: "The dog, the siren and the duck for thirteen pesos." At last, we are delighted to buy the dog for six pesos and just as we walk away we hear the Indian say to the youth: "Tlaloc helped me with the gringos today. Later I am going to bring him two fine ears of corn."

Who could Tlaloc be? We suddenly remember that some four hundred years ago, Tlaloc was the Zapotec rain god. Hunger or a full belly were his doing.

We leave the market thoughtfully and move on to the vast, quiet church square. Whole families of Indians have settled down to eat in the shade of the trees. A dazzling sun shines without mercy on the swarming crowd and the church.

The church tower beckons. Seen from up here, it is a glaringly colorful scene. The market is in an uproar; whoops, shouts, barking and laughter reach us. Scenes of times past appear before our eyes: four hundred and forty years ago, the Zapotecs walked here in long embroidered garments. Vessels dating from their classical period show that they wore fantastic headdresses. Their 22 ft.-long spears were feared everywhere. It has been discovered that their amazing calendar was based on the number of days required for a normal pregnancy. Their religious practices comprised self-mortification, confession for the forgiveness of sins and – within limits – human sacrifice, a practice which we cannot understand.

Up here in the tower we stand on the brink of the unknown and the unrecognizable. Suddenly the bells begin to ring noon in the tower below us. And they ring more quickly than elsewhere as all Mexican bells are in the habit of doing – as if they wanted to cover up, drown out something with their ringing. The unanswerable question remains, nonetheless, whether or not the ancient gods survive tenaciously next to the Christian God deep down in the souls of the Indians.

The ringing has stopped. The hullabaloo of the market place reaches us again. We leave the tower and return to Oaxaca. On the way back, we reach the conclusion that throughout history the church and the market have been the places where men recognize and understand each other.

PULQUE

Greenish-gray, hard, spiked leaves grow from the roots of the maguey plant. They prick and threaten in every direction.

The maguey has thrived in poor soil in Mexico for the last two thousand years. In botany, it is given the name of *agava americana;* it belongs to the Amaryllidaceae. It is as much of a staple in Mexico as corn since it is the source of the most common intoxicating beverage consumed by present-day Mexicans and by their ancestors before them. The honey water, which becomes pulque when fermented, is sucked from the well-protected center of the plant. In Mexico City, on the site where the *zócalo* is today, there was in 1521 an Aztec temple dedicated to the god of pulque. In the vicinity of Tepotzotlán, the Aztecs built a temple dedicated to the god of pulque on the rim of the crater of an enormous volcano. The gods of pulque were lunar beings, half of their faces was painted black, the other half red. They represented the death and rebirth of nature. At harvest time, endless revelries took place in their honor. There are few plants which grow on so little and give so much. The maguey thrives up to an altitude of 8775 ft. In spite of night frosts, burning heat, months without a drop of rain, it is lavish with its water which frequently must replace drinking water in times of drought. Unfermented maguey juice has a sweet and milky taste. It is called *agua miel,* i. e. honey water, and contains vitamins and albumen; fermented, it becomes pulque.

It takes eight years for the maguey to bloom. At that time, the pulque farmer, known as *tlachiquero,* cuts down the shoot and leaves the maguey alone for another four months. Then he cuts into the center of the plant and honey water begins to accumulate near the semi-circular cut. The maguey produces slightly more than two gallons a day for five months; then the plant dies.

Mornings and evenings the *tlachiquero* sucks the honey water from the maguey by means of a gourd perforated at both ends, and pours it into wooden barrels which are carried back to the hacienda. The juice is poured into vats made of cow hides stretched between four posts. The hairy side is turned inwards. The *agua miel* ferments and becomes pulque in twelve hours' time.

Towards evening, after work, when the juice has begun to ferment, the *tlachiqueros* gather in front of the room where the vats are kept, look in and one of them starts to sing a thanksgiving hymn to the Virgin. The others join in the responses. There is a sudden silence. The first man lets out a high piercing scream which lasts for several minutes; then everyone joins in the hymn again. These may still be memories of the Aztec prayer to the god of pulque.

Pulque is the drink of the Mexican people. Anti-alcoholic groups oppose its use, while others try to foster greater consumption of beer. The Indian nonetheless continues to drink pulque on every festive occasion. It permits him to forget quickly and to dream. After all, the Indians used to believe that pulque would flow even in the higher spheres, near the stars. Surely, in their revelries which excluded women, they arrived at a philosophy of drunkenness, as being a completely "different" understanding of the world, as well as an "unconscious," easily acceptable death. No religion could do without its god of drunkenness, of ecstasy.

AZTEC MALINALCO

South of the Toluca highlands, 325 ft. above the village of Malinalco, stands a temple. The mountain on which it rises is wrapped in a bluish haze and shimmers like a landscape in a dream. We leave the village below us and soon find ourselves in front of the temple hewn from the rock. It is the only temple in Mexico which resembles those of the Indian subcontinent and of South Asia.

The mountains around us look like giant lizards with sawed-off tails. Extinct volcanoes and stone bulwarks formed by nature are close by. The Indian village in the small plain below us looks forlorn. The braying of a donkey reaches us and fades. The branches of the banana trees surrounding the village move in the wind, while the prickly pears stand stiffly in the sunlight. Up here there is a slight breeze as if memories of a distant past were stirring in the tree tops.

The pedestal of the temple resembles a pyramid. A flight of stairs leads to the temple entrance; beyond it, there is a circular inner chamber, hewn from the rock. As soon as one sees the low reliefs of two dragon heads at the entrance one has no further doubt about the Aztec origin of the temple. Their brows are sinister and threatening, their teeth mighty, their serpent's tongue is forked. Two stone jaguars guard the stairs. In the sanctuary lie stony relics of flying eagles and jaguars, their lifted tails forever stiffened with rage.

The chronicle mentions this edifice shortly before the landing of the Spaniards and the terrible defeat of the Aztecs – that is, early in the 16th century.

The images hewn into the rock with the most primitive tools by this heroic people conjure up visions of power and of constant threats to it. Now all is peace: only the underbrush moves slightly in the breeze and the ancient stones gleam dully, resting there like legendary animals of prehistoric times.

THE NATIONAL MUSEUM OF ANTHROPOLOGY

Chapultepec Park and its tall trees are situated in the midst of the bustle of Mexico City. The new National Museum of Anthropology rises like a fortress a few steps from the Paseo de la Reforma which cuts through the park.

In a vast courtyard, gay silvery fountains gush from a dark hollow bordered by stones.

Massive white stone blocks frame a low entrance way. A serpent writhing in the talons of the Mexican eagle is hewn from one of them. The coloring and the texture of the stones mitigate the severity of the walls. The entrance hall is monumental and yet not austere. We go past the high glass walls into the enormous, rectangular inner courtyard which is surrounded by three tall wings of the museum. An ornate, gigantic stone pillar supports an inverted free-floating roof. Water rains down from it and condenses into a clear, shiny curtain. The drops explode and round holes in the ground swallow them up.

The steady sound of living water keeps out all the stiffness usually found in museums. The unique rectangular roof which measures 5400 square yards covers part of the patio. Under it, plants grow in still waters which reflect the sky.

Each of the imposing wings is two stories high. Pedro Ramírez Vazquez is the chief architect who looks after this great building.

The halls in which the archaeological collection is housed are on the ground floor, the ethnological collection is on the upper floor: below, the riches of the Mexican past up to colonial times; above, the folklore of the Indian tribes which still exist today. Time and again the eye wanders from the exhibits out to the tall trees and the lawn of the old park and inwards to the peaceful patio.

It takes many hours to visit the whole museum. The objects are drawn from the darkness by beams which illuminate them from above. In the Indian cultures everything had a religious meaning. Their whole life consisted of religious rituals, even power hid under the wing of religion. Seen against the stark blue sky or under the beams of light, the excavated finds seem as mysterious as if the gods still had all of Mexico in their possession. A Maya corn god smiles the unforgettable smile of those who believe that they know the last mysteries, while clear-cut Aztec sculptures threaten cruelly.

We are fascinated by the Teotihuacán masks. They reveal the magic charm of the alter ego. Are we not all one person and yet another? About 400 A.D., during the classical age of Teotihuacán, the stylized mask found its highest expression. This demonic mask dates from the Olmec upheaval. Here there is a mask that frightens, over there a grotesque one with animal traits. What did man to hide at that time? Whom did he wish to deceive or from whom did he seek protection?

Time and again we go out into the sunlit patio and delight in the sound of the water falling from the pillar, from one world into the other.

The upper stories surprise us. Indian huts have been faithfully reproduced in every detail. Indians in their costumes sit in front of them. Huicholes from Nayarit, Mayas from Yucatán, Otomí from Puebla and Zapotecs from Oaxaca were invited to build up their own small world. Life-size dummies of Indians make baskets, fish, weave, hunt, make pottery, cook and work with wood, wax, metal and feathers. Their songs and music played on their instruments are softly piped into the halls. This world of the Indians gives us a strange feeling because of the sudden disappearance of our own world and because of the immediacy with which the "otherness" of this segment of the Mexican population is demonstrated here. Untouched by the colonial period, the Indians have preserved their way of life for the last two thousand years.

We hesitate to leave this wealth of mysteries and insights into the past and the present. Once more we stroll through the halls on the main floor. The temples and their façades, glowing with many bright colors, must have been an incredible sight. Majestic silence now pervades the sacred places from which come the objects exhibited in the museum. A Nahuatl poem is inscribed on one of the patio walls:

We array ourselves with flowers and songs –   And my heart beats joyfully to this day
They are spring flowers.   Because I hear songs and see flowers in bloom.
We array ourselves with them here on earth   O may they never perish.

ACAPULCO

The coastline of Acapulco is luxuriant; one does not expect it to be so as one drives down to the sea and frequently passes through arid regions. The promontories of the bays look like waves. Beyond the mammoth-shaped rocks in the bay, the Pacific is a perfect blue, while closer to the coast it shades off into deep purple. A blue-green haze shimmers above the sea; waves roll in incessantly. When you swim out far into the sea, the palm trees disappear behind the coastline and the mountains look as if they were growing straight out of the sea, while the aluminum colored blocks resemble the fins of prehistoric animals. White clouds meet, join and part again.

Just as in Miami and Palm Beach the air is electrifying. Travellers who know the four corners of the earth say that Acapulco is beyond compare and that it beckons to them again and again.

Hotel thieves, priests, millionaires and dreamers mix in Acapulco. Every day, jets and giant buses bring visitors of all races from all over the world.

The more than fifty thousand inhabitants of this strange town live more or less well on the tourists. They are always on the verge of becoming rich and always end up remaining poor. The architecture is incredible; everyone builds as he pleases. Enormous luxury hotels, small bazaars and elegant bars. Near them, in a backwater, vultures fight over dead animals. All this adds up to a mosaic of the revolting, the enchanting and the unforgettable. Close by, one can find quiet, deserted bays and modest hotels along the beach. Thousands of flowers have been planted everywhere. At noon, the sun blazes down on the clearings in the forest so strongly that it produces hallucinations.

In Acapulco, one experiences a joyfulness one has never known before. In the evening, when the promontories and their purplish waves seem to reach out further into the sea and the lighthouses begin to sparkle under the dark-red sky, it is a moving experience to look down on the peaceful dusky bays. The fishing boats which start up their motors because the wind has died down chug towards the entrance of the bay and these sounds of the active life burst in on our feeling of enchantment. Later, it seems as if the noise of the breakers has died down. As the moon comes up over the cliffs, it obliterates all contrasts. The wild mountains of the coastline stand out beautifully against the night sky.

FIESTA IN CUETZALÁN

Every year, on the 4th of October, the Indians of Cuetzalán celebrate the feast of St. Francis, the local saint. The town is situated at an altitude of 2925 ft. on the steep slopes of the Sierra de Puebla, in the northernmost corner of the state of Puebla. Eight thousand Indians live in the town which, before 1962, was not connected by road with the outside world. Naturally, this isolation helped to preserve beautiful and ancient traditions. On this day, the men wear white shirts, trousers and straw hats. The women – poor though they be – put on white or black long, full skirts, hand-embroidered blouses and belts of particularly attractive workmanship. But it is their headgear which amazes us most. They braid thick, brown or purple woolen strands into their hair so that it becomes a turban-like construction which they carry like queens. The *cuetzalines*, the dancers, have the most beautiful costumes. They wear red ponchos and a 6 ft. "wheel" on their heads; its spokes are made of thin wooden sticks, interwoven with colored paper. At the end of the sticks, there are bright feathers. Nowadays chicken feathers are used, but in the past they were the long, green tail feathers of the mystically venerated quetzal bird. The dance is of pre-Columbian origin. They also dance a story about a snake, whose meaning is no longer known. The *toritos,* the young Indians, bring out stands covered with fire crackers which are dispatched with deafening noise.
There is no end to the celebrations. Religous customs, be they Christian or pagan, co-exist amicably.
Each Mexican village and town has its own saint and he has a name day to be observed each year, so that all year round, somewhere in Mexico, a saint's day is celebrated with much rejoicing and wholehearted devotion.

JOURNEY TO PUEBLA

The car travels quietly and smoothly. The road sign on the Mexico City – Puebla highway shows that the distance between the two cities is about 80 miles. We are going slowly in order to take in a vast landscape – on the horizon, one line joins another; later on, one mountain range merges into another. Lonely forests clamber up and down the mountain sides and in this enormous space framed by cumulus clouds, the Mexican landscape composed of plains and mountain ranges, silence and vastness, unfolds in front of us. We are dazzled by the two volcanoes, Ixtaccihuatl and Popocatepetl. Their snow-capped peaks sparkle in the sunlight and their foothills slowly lose themselves in the plain – as if they were dragging green trains behind them. We stop at some breathtaking look-out points along the way. The two giants rise in melancholy grandeur as if to proclaim the innermost power of the earth. In the past, lava flowed from them and the hot ashes made the soil fertile.

The first impression which strikes us in Puebla is the light, colorful cheerfulness of its rectilinear streets. In the center of one of the largest cities in Mexico (346,000 inhabitants) one finds store upon store and many perpendicular signs displaying advertisements. Frequently one comes across modern shops with glass fronts built into old houses which have retained the colonial style in the upper stories. We are surrounded by provincial bustle. The faded brown and gray awnings which shade the balconies are particularly attractive. A fountain built during the colonial period spouts water in the *zócalo*. In 1777, the Spaniards placed on the pedestal the statue of a warrior forcing wild animals into an iron chain. The cathedral, a huge, sturdy and compact building, rises next to the *zócalo*. It looks like a bulwark against uncertainty and impermanence. It was built by Francisco Becera during the reign of Philip the Second of Spain. Construction began in 1575. The style in which the portals and the twin towers were conceived is restrained. Red and yellow tiles sparkle on the spires, while green and yellow tiles glisten on the central cupola and the light at certain hours makes it look as if it had been dipped into greenish gold. The façade bears the insignias of the Golden Fleece.

It is cool inside. It took the Spaniards and their vassals 115 years to finish the building. It was inaugurated in 1665 by a powerful Spanish bishop, Juan de Palafox y Mendoza. The silence is shattered by the powerful bell in the tower.

The *coro* disrupts the nave; it is reserved for the priests. Montañes designed the royal altar in the apse. Puebla onyx has been used everywhere. We are told about the Thorn of Christ kept behind the bishop's throne in the choir stalls. The Oaxacan artist, Miguel Cabrera, painted the fourteen stations of the Cross, instilling them with a new life.

Then we stroll through the streets and take time to pause now and again in front of tiled colonial houses.

The church dignitary who inaugurated the cathedral also founded the Biblioteca Palafoxiana in 1646. Fifty thousand volumes representing the sum of knowledge of that time are at the reader's disposal. Incunabula and leather-bound works fill three floors. The bookcases and galleries are made of precious cedar wood. Euclid, Xenophon and a bearded Plato look down serenely from above. The reading tables in the middle of the room have tops made of onyx. We return quietly to the street through corridors paved with red tiles, well-worn by three centuries.

An Indian sits in front of the entrance with several tiny birds. They sit on a branch and don't fly away because their wings are clipped. In spite of the noise of the buses, they seem to be absorbed by the call of a wild pigeon near by.

Wherever we go, we see churches with tiled twin towers among the houses lining the streets. Supposedly there are sixty of them. Puebla has the reputation of being the most religious city in Mexico. It was founded in 1531 by the Spaniards because a Dominican saw two angels hovering above the site in a dream. The city proudly calls itself the "site of the angels." It is halfway between Veracruz and Mexico City. Nowadays it is an agricultural, fruit-growing and textile center. Large industries are developing in the Puebla plain.

A white monument in the *zócalo* reminds us of a battle which took place at the gates of the city. On the 5th of May 1862, two thousand indignant Mexicans defeated a French army of six thousand men there. Mexico fought for its freedom once more. Under Juarez (this Zapotec Indian, who became president, wisely said: "Respect the rights of others and there will be peace.") liberal Mexicans fought French troups who wanted to make a French colony of their country. General Porfirio Diaz, who later became president, distinguished himself in the battle of Puebla. Since then, the 5th of May is a national holiday and many streets have been named for that date.

Glazed tiles sparkle everywhere, the most beautiful are deep blue or persimmon yellow. They have been used on fountains and benches, they cover cupolas, shine from secular buildings and brighten up the city.

We step into another church, Santo Domingo. The exterior gives no hint of the glorious interior. The gilded center altar piece is an example of the plateresque style. There are eighteen niches containing statues of saints and glass cases crowd each other on the left and on the right in wild Churrigueresque style. Near the entrance, an organ clings to the wall near the choir loft as if it were a bird's nest.

The Chapel of the Rosary opens towards the left. For a split second, we don't believe our eyes. Every type of architecture offers a point on which the eye can come to rest. There is no such hold here, the eye can only glide on and on. Apart from the planes formed by the large, time-darkened portraits by Rodríguez Carnero, the ceiling and the walls are covered with gilded ornaments that intertwine, link, mesh and push forth medaillons from which naive cherubs, angels and saints look down fixedly. Laughing cherubs clamber upwards through gilded stucco vines. Light and shadow have been orchestrated. Although the ornaments tend to soar, they give the impression of being massive and heavy. Suddenly we remember the *alcázar* in Seville and the impression left by the Moorish stucco work. Nonetheless this florid ornamentation is powerful. The chapel was designed in Baroque style with Mudéjar overtones by Augustín Hernandez, a Dominican monk. About 1660, the Dominicans gave a free hand to the Indian workmen who completed it ca. 1690.

A statue of the Virgin stands on the Rosary altar. She is the patroness of pearl fishers. Her rosy garment is stiffly starched and covered by a blue cloak; she holds the child tenderly. Every pillar on her altar looks like a spiral winding upwards. The top angel wears the words "Ave Maria" like a decoration across his chest. The Chapel of the Rosary was called "the eighth wonder of the world" by an admirer.

TEPOTZOTLÁN

The western façade of the Jesuit church in Tepotzotlán gleams like ivory in the late afternoon sun. Its bell tower, which is next to the church on the right, is as ornate near the top as the façade of the church itself which is covered by a creeper-like stone tangle – as if stone had become weightless and a plaything of the imagination. In the middle of the 18th century, Spanish Churrigueresque attained heights in Mexico which it never reached in Europe; the ideas of Balbás and Rodriguez were translated into reality.

A precocious-looking Infant Jesus cheerfully gazes into the distance from the middle of the façade; the small globe in its hand looks like a toy. Separated from him only by ivory-colored curtains, a worried God the Father holds a similar globe surmounted by a small cross. On all three levels, laughing cherubs crowd towards him and cheerfully puff up their cheeks. Volutes, arches and columns look like sign posts. Cherub heads hold flower garlands in their mouths. Stone plants fade into the wall on both sides. The jungle could have inspired some of the ornaments. Wainscoting, consoles, cornices, corners and spirals confront the eye. In niches between them stand sumptuous statues of saints, ladies and ladylike angels. Way at the top, a figure points to the clouds.

This monastery was founded by the Jesuits, undoubtedly with the intention of converting the Indians who lived around it. Nowadays it has become the well-known National Museum of Colonial Art.

In the entrance of the museum there is a map of the whole monastery: it consists of four patios, three chapels, a church, a library and many cells. The imposing exterior makes us want to see the Baroque interior.

The first chapel, the one in which the novices knelt, gets its light from two small windows which resemble portholes. The nave is covered – overloaded – with gilded Baroque altars, reliquaries, statues of saints, columns, volutes and pilasters. The various missionary orders which arrived in Mexico shortly after the Conquest are listed on the ceiling: the Franciscans, the Dominicans, the Augustines, the Jesuits and the Carmelites. The most delightful features of this hybrid décor are two ladies on the left of the nave. Their rococo charm is enchanting. They tempt one into believing that gracefulness and naiveté lead straight to heaven.

The big church is dedicated to St. Martin; St. Francis Xavier, the brave and faithful follower of St. Ignatius of Loyola stands on the main altar. To the right of the altar piece, St. Ignatius himself concentrates on his spiritual exercises since he knows full well what a source of courageous obedience and spiritual power they are. Churriguera, who never visited Mexico, would have been amazed by the ecstatic opulence achieved by his style under the influence of the Indians.

The next chapel, the Loretto chapel, is closed. We go on to the *camerino,* the room reserved for the garments and jewels of the Virgin. At first it looks like a frozen, golden cascade. Indian caryatides, painted black, eye us wildly from the corners of the room, but bear their baskets of fruit gently. Unwittingly our glance is drawn to the uppermost lantern where a dove, the ancient symbol of the Holy Spirit, is suspended. It reflects the colors which surround it up there: old gold, blood red, hortensia blue and reddish-gold. Everything is full of exuberance and yet, elegance, imagination and élan manage to blend into a harmonious whole.

Outside the chapel, we see two oils by the celebrated Miguel Cabrera. He was a good artist. His self-portrait and his oil of Juana Inés de la Cruz in Mexico City should not be missed, they are excellent examples of 18th-century painting. It was Cabrera who founded the first academy of painting in Mexico City in 1735.

After the three chapel museums, we must also look at certain individual works of art. A wealth of Baroque painting, sculpture and religious folk art is displayed in some of the monastery halls. A pleasant touch: concealed loudspeakers pipe in music by Vivaldi.

From the window one can see a cloister with two cisterns. There is a polychrome Christ, nailed to a tree, which may well have been fashioned by Indian hands. The delicate blending of colors in a portrait of St. Theresa of Avial, painted by Nicolas Rodríguez at the beginning of the 18th century, amazes us. We shall long remember its purples and soft greens. A polychrome, life-size, Baroque sculpture by an anonymous artist representing St. Francis was brought here from the San Diego convent. From the window one can look out on a cloister with arcades in which many trees grow.

Art treasures were brought to Tepotzotlán from all over Mexico. A very original wooden sculpture carved in the 18th century stands against the far wall of one of the halls. The artist has taken a cylindrical section of an enormous tree. He has carved a niche into it which is painted bright blue, gold, crimson, brick-red and green. In it, Christ is falling under the burden of the Cross while looking straight at us. It would be too easy to dismiss it as primitive folk art. The power of an unconditional, childlike faith radiates from it and it is this faith which has drawn a small miracle from a block of wood. Below the figure of Christ sit the four evangelists with their attributes. In a fury of inspiration they write with enormous goose quills in a large book spread across their knees. Their ecstasy has made their cloaks flare out behind them so that they mingle with the wall of the niche. Their emotion is so great that they bend forward very far while they write and their eyes look beyond their book into chasms, beyond the Divine Word.

To be sure, the whole carving is clumsy, inelegant, without technique, yet our spoiled taste must admit that it is an enchanting representation of the Christian message because art is always simultaneously "vision, explosion, discipline and transformation."

It is getting dark outside and still the visitors continue to arrive. Entire families walk – almost tiptoe – through "their monastery." Now the façade looks like gray moiré silk; the shadows enhance its blurred charm. A large yellow butterfly alights on the globe held by the Infant Jesus.

THE MEXICO CITY CATHEDRAL

It looks as if the *zócalo* had been swept clean by a storm or by powerful voices. It is even larger than the Red Square in Moscow. The Mexico City cathedral on the north side dominates it as a matter of course. Its two towers have bell-shaped stone hats similar to those of certain manor houses. Beneath them many bronze bells call to Divine Worship. The façade gives an impression of cool restraint; there are some severe Renaissance elements in it and the stone acanthus leaves never lose their stiffness. It is an imposing and powerful structure built in the course of two and a half centuries to be the church of the conquerors. It is an archiepiscopal mother-church, the largest in the Americas. The corner stone was laid in 1573, it was finished in 1813.

In an earlier age, the *teocalli,* the brightly colored temples of the mighty Aztecs had been erected on this site. The Spaniards tore them down in 1521 and first built on that very spot a Romanesque church in which the victors sang hymns of jubilation. The stones sculpted by the Aztecs were used for the foundations of the cathedral which was built there later and which was dedicated to the

Assumption of the Virgin. Proud eagles hover over the portals. The doric interior preserves its cold decorum even when it is filled with clouds of incense and the loud prayers of the priests and when hundreds of young mothers bring their crying babies to be baptized. The two enormous organs which hang high above the *coro* have been silent for a long time. Soft light falls into the vast interior through new, honey-colored windows designed by Mathias Göritz and gives it a somewhat warmer feeling. We are fascinated by a massive altar piece in the north apse which is 88 ft. high and covered entirely with gold leaf. This was the first example of Baroque art in Mexico, designed in the 18th century by Jerónimo de Balbas from Seville, and it became the point of departure for the Churrigueresque style which was used on a large scale in hundreds of churches throughout the country. This altar piece is dedicated to the kings who vigorously defended their church. The queens are represented in the lower part, the kings in the upper, and the King of Kings in the center.

We stroll on and admire the seventy-four arches in the five naves which rest on walls 8 ft. wide. Fifty cupolas form the ceiling.

Near the portals there is another Baroque altar. Two angels carrying bunches of flowers hasten towards the crown which glitters at the top. The graceful and fervent St. Sebastian was painted in the 17th century by Echave the Elder, a Spanish artist. Below him hangs a portrait of the Mother of all Grace. According to legend, the Flemish artist S. Berynes, who had been entrusted with the task of painting a religious picture, blasphemed and was therefore imprisoned. One morning the guard who brought him his food was astonished to find this portrait of the Virgin on the door of the cell. It still has a special radiance. The light which falls through the windows gilds a spider way up high as he spins golden threads from one point of the crown to another.

Some of the fourteen side chapels have been decorated recently; others are very old. All the paintings in the Angel Chapel, the first one on the left near the entrance, were painted by Juán Correa in 1714. There is a Murillo in the sacristy.

Our attention is attracted by a baptismal font behind a wooden grill; according to an inscription, the only Mexican saint, San Felipe de Jésus, was baptized with its Holy Water. He was crucified in 1597 in Nagasaki because of his missionary zeal. Recently, delicate frescoes were discovered in the Cuernavaca cathedral which represent scenes from his life and martyrdom. When there is silence in the cathedral, the faithful can hear the splashing of water in the baptismal font.

The sun blinds us as we leave the cathedral. It shines on the light-gray cobble stones of the *zócalo* around which there is heavy traffic. The fascinating Churrigueresque façade of the *Sagrario* (sanctuary) adjoins that of the cathedral. It is covered with a wealth of decorative elements. One could best describe it by saying that it is a stone altar turned outwards. Lorenzo Rodríguez, a Spaniard, built it between 1749 and 1768; he used red volcanic stone.

We go to the middle of the square where we can be completely by ourselves since the traffic is confined to its outskirts.

In 1325, when the Aztecs fled from persecutions in the north, their priests saw on this island – the *zócalo* was an island at that time – an eagle sitting on a cactus with a serpent in its talons. They took this to be a sign from the gods and they settled here. Since then, the eagle with a serpent in its talons has been emblazoned on the Mexican coat of arms. This site became the center of Aztec ascendancy; here they built their colorful temples and held their markets. It is on this very spot, saturated with their sacrifices, that they were decisively defeated by the Spaniards in 1521. After that, the gallows of the Spaniards seldom remained unoccupied. As early as 1522, the conquerors used Aztec temple stones to build a Romanesque church on this spot and from then on, they celebrated their victory each year on the 13th of August. The first bull fights were held in the *zócalo* in 1526 and, soon after, the first trials of the Inquisition. The Mexican people had to win their independence by several bloody rebellions. The Spanish flag was raised above this square for centuries; the American flag flew above it in 1847 and the French flag in 1863. On the east side the whole length of the *zócalo* is taken up by the seat of the government, the National Palace. On the south side, across from the cathedral, are the large municipal buildings whose construction was decreed by Charles the Fifth. The square is all sobriety and seriousness in spite of the cheerful sky above it.

On September 15th, 1810, Miguel Hidalgo y Costilla, the pastor of the small town of Dolores in the north of Mexico, rang the bells of his church and called upon the assembled Indians and mestizos to fight for their liberation. Thus the struggle for freedom under the banner of Our Lady of Guadalupe began. It took 110 years of fighting the enemy within and without to achieve it. Every year on September 15th, the *zócalo* is so tightly packed with humanity that no one can move. The president rings the liberty bell and the heart of every Mexican beats faster when he repeats the outcry of Dolores: "Viva Mexico!"

TLALTELOLCO, MEXICO CITY

Nothing in Tlaltelolco has been deliberately planned and yet it looks like a stage set. Blocks of stones, walls and flights of stairs leading nowhere have been excavated from the damp clay in front of St. James Church. Destroyed pyramids, temple remains, ruined palaces and sunken graveyards were found in the five layers which have been excavated. An intricate network of past ages was discovered while the foundations for a new residential section were being laid. The archaeologists have proved that this was the site of the ancient Tlaltelolco, a citadel and sanctuary district which was surrounded by canals. The chronicles tell us that this city on the lagoons put up the longest and most embittered resistance to the onslaught of the Spaniards. A whole civilization succumbed here. A touching commemorative plaque reads as follows: "Tlaltelolco fell into the hands of Hernándo Cortés on the 13th of August 1521. It was defended heroically by Cuauhtemoc. It was neither a victory nor a defeat. It was the painful birth of a people of mestizos, of the Mexico of today."

The Tepanecs had consolidated Tlaltelolco, their island on Texcoco lake, by adding soil to it. Before that, the lake flooded their houses each year during the rainy season. It wasn't until 1475 that they became the vassals of the Aztec warriors. The Tlaltelolco market continued to be an important trading post where the richest merchants met. There were two stately pyramids crowned by colorful temples on the site on which the archaeologists now try to reconstruct the past. The Tlaltelolco merchants monopolized the trade with other peoples and lent money on interest. The currency consisted of cacao beans in units of twenty or bales of 8000 beans. Large sums were paid with quills filled with gold. Cortés and Bernal Díaz saw the market with their own eyes and Cortés wrote that it was twice as large as that of Salamanca in Spain. It was surrounded by arcades where the market police kept careful watch. Rich merchants served as judges for the trials which were held in the center of the market place. Each type of merchandise was assigned a specific location in the market. Father Sahagún, the Spanish chronicler, mentioned merchants dealing in sixty different types of goods. The slave merchants were, of course, the most wealthy. The Tepanecs and the Aztecs were forbidden by law to demolish any of the temples or ceremonial buildings. When 52 years – an "age" according to their calendar – had gone by without a major catastrophy, the old buildings were encased in other constructions, which helps to explain the flights of stairs leading nowhere on the excavation site.

Places such as this still seem to ring with history even though the dynamic present is all around us. Behind us, on a high bridge made of concrete the traffic of the capital rushes by. A maze of excavations lies before us; beyond it, to the left, one sees the modest Church of St. James, and to the right, the Colegio Santa Cruz in which the offspring of the subjugated Aztec nobility were introduced to the "new God." The Spaniards made a point of building on the sites which "belonged" to the pagan gods.

Every year on the 25th of July, groups of Indians dance in the square on the north side of the church to express their reverence for the saint. The new faith taught by the Franciscans probably seemed like a new dawn to the Aztecs since it brought them deliverance from the demonic powers which ruled them. The spirit of these powers still survives in the cemeteries; it speaks in the broken pottery and is witnessed by the stones. For centuries, various populations sacrificed the blood of their children and their enemies on these altars to overcome the powers of darkness. History obliterated their travail, their pleasures, their battles and their enthusiasms. During four centuries the Spaniards and the vanquished Indians mingled and thus – in sorrow – the Mexican people was born; it reached its maturity when it shook off the foreign yoke in the 19th century. The past is a precious part of every Mexican. These ruins are shrouded in the mystery of former greatness. It seems almost symbolical that the new Ministry for Foreign Affairs has been built right next to the excavation site.

This spot, where an end was put to the Aztec era by the Spanish-Christian era, has been named "The square of the three cultures." Which is the third, the new culture? Perhaps it is particularly manifest here where a residential section for 60,000 inhabitants shop up in two short years. A tall, pyramidal bell tower made of glass competes with the church tower, it houses the administration of this development, as well as two banks. Yellow apartment houses, white apartment towers, low, earth-colored school buildings, gardens and more than a thousand trees make up this housing project which cost one and a half billion pesos. The gap between reality and desirability is very tangible here. All that has been achieved in gathering together 60,000 people is that they have been given decent housing, but what our age should try to achieve is decentralization and closeness to nature.

THE VIRGIN OF GUADALUPE

Pigeons suddenly fly up past the scaffoldings into the cupola of the magnificent basilica of Our Lady of Guadalupe and quietly return to perch below. The statue of the Virgin, surrounded by a sea of pink and white gladiolas, is kept behind glass on the main altar. She is dark-skinned, like many of the worshippers at her feet. Everyone kneels, everyone responds to the prayer recited by a priest at one of the side altars. Loudspeakers hang from the pillars; some boom, others just hum. Whenever a space becomes vacant, women begin to inch up the center aisle on their knees, closer and closer to the Virgin. They cross themselves and recite litanies, always with the same inflection. Even the name of the Virgin is invoked in the same monotonous tone, the way it has been spoken innumerable times since childhood. At the Elevation even the people standing near the entrance fall to their knees. Their clothes rustle like the wind. Those who are close to the Virgin spread out their arms if they were offering their hearts.

We return to the enormous square in front of the basilica. Since it is built on swamp land, it has sunk slightly below street level and the presbytery has followed suit. The square is peaceful; an iron fence surrounds it. We are touched by the sight of three children sliding towards us on their knees, inch after inch. Just behind them a whole family slowly does the same; their knees are already bloody. The wires on the flagpoles are beating loudly in the wind, iron against iron.

On Saturday, the 12th of December 1531, an Indian by the name of Juan Diego was on his way to catechism class in the vicinity of the capital. A dark-skinned Virgin appeared to him. When he told the bishop about the apparition, her picture suddenly appeared on his coarsely woven shoulder cloth and when he spread it out – dumbfounded and afraid – dewy roses fell into it. Father Juan de Zumárraga, the bishop, immediately ordered the construction of a chapel near the site of the apparition and the miraculous picture of the Virgin of Guadalupe was displayed on the altar. It was the very spot on which, until the Conquest, the Aztecs had venerated Tonantzín, the goddess of fertility. The word Guadalupe comes from the Aztec word Coaxtlazore and signifies "the one who crushed the serpent under her foot."

After that, the Spanish missionaries met with greater cooperation. Between 1521 and 1531, not quite a million Indians had reluctantly agreed to embrace Christianity. After the 12th of December 1531, when their dark-skinned goddess appeared to one of their own, they accepted conversion more readily. Seven million Indians were baptized in the next few years. Today the Virgin of Guadalupe is the patroness of Mexico. In and outside Mexico, 421 churches are dedicated to her. Her picture on Juan Diego's shoulder cloth has remained unharmed. Until 1666, hundreds of pilgrims kissed it every day, after that it was put under glass for protection. A time bomb exploded in front of it in 1920 at the time of the religious persecutions by the Mexican government. A heavy bronze cross was twisted by the explosion, marble blocks fell, a statue of St. Nepomuk was destroyed, but the picture of the Virgin remained unharmed. The basilica was the only church to remain open even at that time when all the other churches in Catholic Mexico had been closed. On the Feast of Christ the King in 1927, more than 200,000 Mexicans assembled around the church. They were led by a Jesuit, Miguel Pro, who was later executed. The anti-religious government was powerless. Millions would have had to be sent to prison had they tried to cut off the Mexicans from their patroness.

Every year, on the day commemorating her apparition, thousands flock to her from all over Mexico. They often come incredible distances on foot. She is the Saint, the Virgin, the Mother and the Queen of the Indians and in a way they attach greater importance to her than to Christ. For hours – as if possessed – they dance their ancient dances in the Plaza de las Americas, the square in front of the basilica. They sleep, cook, eat and pray on the stone slabs of the square. They spend days there and sometimes they secretly call the Virgin "Tonantzín." All year round pilgrims visit the Virgin, factory workers offer her presents, taxi drivers have their cars blessed, animals are brought to her. Those who seek, those who do penance, those who are ill, they all come to her in search of peace.

When we look at the tear-stained faces of the faithful who approach the Virgin of Guadalupe, we realize that they experience the presence of the absolute mystery in this religious symbol. Moreover they long to reach out beyond their own limited nature once a year. When the Mexicans bow before the picture of the Virgin and quietly leave the basilica, they see a new meaning in their own world. They take their joy home with them to be guarded like a precious light.

We stop one more time in front of the Virgin. She is touchingly helpless in the midst of all the ostentatious decorations. The limitless affection bestowed upon her gives us an idea of what early Christendom must have been. The pilgrims return from here to their everyday lives both relieved and fortified against destiny.

ESPERANTO LESSONS IN CHAPULTEPEC PARK

As soon as a slight breeze stirs, a cloud of colorful balloons strains upwards toward the sunny sky which beckons to them. Wherever we look on this Sunday morning – close by, behind trees, off into the distance – we see men holding clouds of balloons. The park is overrun with people today. They laugh, sit, walk about, run, eat and generally populate the vast, tree-shaded expanse. The green of the lawn is dotted by women's colorful dresses: lots of ochre, orange and green, but scarlet predominates. The faces run the gamut from yellow to coffee. The wide sombreros conceal the faces of the men almost completely. It is a colorful, lively crowd: small employees walking their children, workers, artisans, maids, civil servants – the curious, the idle, those who want to find a seat, those who seek a quiet spot, people who laugh, whistlers, people in wheel chairs, people who like to watch the world go by. Everyone is cheerful; they call to one another, greet each other, laugh, curse or remain silent. The old ahuehuete trees shade them against the sun; occasionally its rays pierce the leafy roof and reach right down to the enormous roots. They all enjoy themselves naively, they don't seem to have a care in the world.

A band plays a lively tune. The sound fades and suddenly booms forth again. A dense crowd has gathered around the music pavilion. Young men put on a show of heroism as they row their girls across the lake. Whole families rock gently in boats. Some of them seem a little frightened although the boats look as if they couldn't possibly sink.

Over there, a group of women and young girls crowd around a table. They manipulate each others' heads and hands and all of them wear curlers in loud colors. An awkwardly lettered inscription on a blackboard hanging from a tree announces that this is a "Beauty salon." They are all "crowned" in the same fashion. One girl carefully massages another girl's face with cream; a woman draws eyebrows on another; the scent of hair lotion and a sharper smell of nail polish surrounds them; a girl kneels on the ground while someone carefully arranges her hair. We look at every one of them. They are too absorbed in their own pursuits to pay attention to us. The onlookers, the park, the sun and the music all go unnoticed as they enjoy beautifying themselves.

Some 15 ft. beyond them, men of all ages sit on wooden benches in front of an ahuehuete tree and listen closely to a young man who slowly pronounces English words for them. He repeats each word three times. The blackboard on the tree says "English I." They write the words into blue note-books held on their knees. Some of them form the letters very carefully, others jot them down, cross them out and patiently start all over again. The young teacher only sees the dark eager eyes which stare at him as if he were teaching them something more essential than the rudiments of the English language.

Who could have thought up this humanitarian scheme and – what is more – who could actually have managed to carry it out? Men and women of all ages have lined up in front of a wobbly table a few steps from us. We learn from the young man behind it that for the last six months, two teachers, a husband and wife, have simply approached other teachers and asked them whether they would be willing to give lessons here on Sunday mornings. They teach without salary. "And now we can barely supply the demand," he says beamingly, as he points at the line. "Basically, the idea was due to the great desire of the illiterate to acquire some learning. It is only on Sundays that they have time and the strength to learn to read and to write." He points to a table around which there are only old people and says: "They are learning the alphabet." This form of social action will bring many rewards.

We go eagerly from table to table, from one small group to another. Over here, a stocky man teaches bookbinding; there, women make animals out of scraps of material; further on a woman doctor instructs her group in First Aid; not far from her, a large group is taking in the basic principles of electrical engineering. There is always a blackboard propped against a tree trunk which indicates what subject is being taught. A very decided woman teaches a group of housemaids how to vary their sauces. An aroma of thyme and onion hangs in the air. Men learn to plane wood under a flowering tree. The shavings mingle with the white blossoms to form a light blanket on the ground. A sewing machine rests on the gnarled roots of an ancient ahuehuete tree; three girls are learning to sew on it at once. A few steps from them young people perform a folk dance from northern Mexico. In another group, a teacher calls an older man to the blackboard and asks him to write six zeros behind a one so that it will become a million. He hesitates, puts down the chalk and leaves the task to a younger man. The sign near them reads "Mathematics I." Lacquer work, stenography, crochet work, English II, tailoring – there is no end to what the willing can learn.

Off to one side, a small group of men and women has gathered closely around a tree. We stop next to an Indian woman with long, white braids who is easily over seventy to find out what subject is being taught here. Her grandson, who looks exactly like her, stands next to her. The blackboard is hidden by the group. The teacher sounds foreign. It must be a language class – but certainly not an Indian dialect. At this point, someone sits down and through the gap we see that the sign says "Esperanto I" in blue chalk.

It is amazing how absorbed people of all ages are. First they repeat the words reverently, then they lower their heads and painstakingly write them into their notebooks with their calloused hands, their foreheads wrinkled with effort. Their fervent concentration shows how greatly they long for knowledge.

The music grows louder. A breeze stirs in the old trees and we sit down to rest on a sun-warmed bench, off to the side.

EXPLANATION OF PHOTOGRAPHS

End papers. The Cuernavaca cathedral was built by the Franciscans in 1529 at the order of Cortés. In 1952, during a renovation, frescoes were discovered on the north wall and carefully brought to light. They were painted in the middle of the 17th century to honor San Felipe de Jesús, the only Mexican saint. He and twenty-five Franciscan monks went to Japan as missionaries in 1597 and were executed in Nagasaki.

1 On the road to Estecas in the state of Morelos. Organ cactus.

2 On the Gulf coast, archaeologists found remnants of a civilization thought to have flourished about 200 B.C. It remains a mystery how the Olmecs, i.e. the people from the rubber country, were able to bring stones for their sculptures weighing fifty tons from a distance of some 80 miles to their jungle city. A figure holding roped prisoners sits in the niche of an Olmec altar. Above it, a stylized jaguar. The Olmec civilization was still close to nature since it was not too far removed in time from the archaic period.

3 According to the German archaeologist Krickeberg, this gigantic monolithic head is "one of the most amazing works of Meso-American sculpture." It was found in the middle of the jungle, in a mangrove swamp, on an island in the state of Tabasco. It wears a tight-fitting cap with straps across the forehead and the chin. Today it stands, some eight feet high, in La Venta Park in Villa Hermosa. It was not part of a human body originally, but rested, bodyless even then, on a base in front of the Olmec sanctuary.

4–5 Teotihuacán, the sacred city, lies about 32 miles north of Mexico City. Only remnants of this civilization can still be seen. View from the south side of the Pyramid of the Moon down the Via Sacra, the Highway of the Dead, which is straight as an arrow; it leaves the Pyramid of the Sun to the left and is bordered on both sides by small pyramids. The Swedish archaeologist Linné discovered that this highway runs 17 degrees east of due north so that, on two days of the year, the east-west axis meets the horizon at the very point at which the sun seems to disappear into the earth. This shows how well the Teotihuacáns had acquired and applied a knowledge of astronomy without the help of any optical instruments. Teotihuacán flourished from 100 B.C. to 350 A.D. approximately. See text, p. 10.

6   View of the sunny courtyard of the Butterfly Temple in Teotihuacán. The golden age of this sanctuary was about 350 A.D. Restored pillars with carved butterflies, quetzal birds and shells. The animals are the symbols of the rain god. See text, p. 11.

7   Teotihuacán. The famous temple of Quetzalcoatl is located in the inner courtyard of a plaza named the *Ciudadela.* Serpent heads decorate the façade. There is a relief of plumed serpents on the pedestal. It is a powerful structure. See text, p. 11.

8   Pyramid of the Moon in Teotihuacán. Its base is rectangular (426 x 511 ft., height 150 ft.). It faces southward. There is a single flight of stairs interrupted by platforms. See text, p. 10, 11.

9   A brightly colored fresco representing the rain god was found in a house in Atetlita in Teotihuacán. Water runs from his hands. See text, p. 11.

10   A lava field between Ixtapán and Cuernavaca. State of Morelos.

11   Indian woman from Toluca. State of Mexico.

12–13   Palenque. The Maya ruins are situated in the heart of the rain forest of the Usamacinta river in the state of Chiapas. We don't even know their real name. Palenque was the name given to them by the Spaniards. See text, p. 12.

14   Temple of the Cross in the Maya sanctuary in Palenque which is entirely surrounded by dense jungle. On its roof there is a *Crestería,* a crest-like frontispiece which used to be covered with stucco reliefs. See text, p. 12, 13.

15   This beautiful Maya relief is kept in the Palenque Museum. It may represent a servant turned towards a god. The bridge of his nose is built up artificially. Sculptures such as these show why the Mayas were called the "Greeks" of the American continent. See text, p. 12.

16   The Chamulas are an Indian tribe which lives in dispersed settlements in the state of Chiapas in southern Mexico. They are a short, yellowish-brown people and speak a tongue which belongs to the family of Maya languages. The Government makes great efforts to promote their welfare. This photograph shows three camera-shy Chamula women in flight. They carry earthen jugs with the help of forehead bands.

17 San Cristobal de las Casas in Chiapas. This Chamula was laughing because his picture was being taken. The shape of his hat is traditional among the Chamulas. His clothing consists of two rectangular pieces of woollen cloth sewn together lengthwise so as to leave openings for the arms and short, trouser-like cloths around the thighs.

18 The Tula river. Organ cactus in the foreground. A wild, arid landscape typical of the sparsely inhabited Mexican mountains.

19 Remains of the Temple of the Morning Star in Tula, the main Toltec sanctuary north of the capital, which was built between 800 and 1100 A.D. Giant Atlas-like figures (15 ft. high) used to carry the roof of the temple. The warriors are dressed in the Toltec costume, stylized butterflies on their chests, arms to their sides, spears in their hands; their faces are severe. Awe-inspiring even today.

20 The Maya sanctuary in Kabah was founded in 879 A.D. near the Uxmal temple district in Yucatan. During the 11th and 12th centuries, the Kabah area was densely populated. The three groups of buildings which have been excavated are in the late Maya style and show the influence of the Toltecs from the highlands of Mexico. This plate represents the Palace of Masks. Bizarre, trunk-nosed masks of Chac, the Maya god, are repeated along the entire 150 ft. façade.

21 Maya ruins in Uxmal, Yucatán. A long, center building, extended further by two wings, stands on a 588 ft. long terrace. See text, p. 14.

22 North wing of the Nunnery in Uxmal. The Temple of Venus with a portico and four columns stands in front of it. The mosaic-like decorations are fanciful and geometrical. See text, p. 15.

23 Maya ruins in Uxmal, Yucatán. Many additions were made to the House of the Magician. Five times temples were erected on the various terraces from which the structure slowly grew.
See text, p. 14.

24 Each day during harvest time, Indian women bring oranges for sale to the village of Ticul in Yucatan. They wear long, stark-white Maya shirts with colorful, hand-embroidered trimmings.

25   The caracol in Chichén Itzá, Yucatan. The two-story tower served as an observatory; it stands on a 41 ft. high platform with two terraces. The name *caracol* was given to it because of the resemblance of a small spiral staircase in the tower to a snail shell. During a survey, slits were discovered in the walls which permitted the observation of celestial bodies. The Mayas and the Aztecs obtained surprisingly precise results in astronomy without the aid of optical instruments. In the Codex Mendoza one finds priests observing the sky. In the field of astronomy, this civilization surpassed all other contemporary knowledge.

26   Ball court in Chichén Itzá, Yucatan. There are carvings on all the enclosure walls. The ball player on the left has decapitated the ball player on the right and holds up his head. The beheaded man sinks to his knees to the right of the disk. Six spurts of blood spring from his neck, become six snakes, which in turn are transformed into blossoms and fruit, symbolizing the fruitfulness of sacrifice.

27   Ball court in the Maya sanctuary of Chichén Itzá, Yucatan, about 900 A.D. Surprisingly enough, many Indian tribes in Mexico built such courts in their holy places. They were not intended for sports, but for deadly confrontations. It is probable that these matches were meant to symbolize sunrise and sunset. Presumably the two teams competed by throwing a four and a half pound solid rubber ball through the perpendicular stone ring attached to the wall. The losers paid with their lives. The greatest difficulty of the game was that the ball could only be touched with the elbows and the hips. This ceremonial game can only be understood as a kind of magic by analogy. In the foreground, on the right, one sees the very ornate temple of the caste of the jaguar warriors.

28   In front of the Temple of the Warriors in Chichén Itzá lies the stone figure of a god. His head is turned sidewards and he holds a cup. His Maya name is Chac Mool. He is supposed to have taken the gifts of mankind to the gods. His glance is strange, even mysterious, as he looks out into space.

29   Temple of the Warriors in Chichén Itzá, Yucatan. A plumed serpent with gaping mouth lies at the bottom of the starcase which leads to the Temple of Kukulcan (height 78 ft.). In front of the temple there are incredibly vast procession roads. One can see the whole front of the Temple of the Warriors crowned by the sanctuary in which the sacrifices were offered. Pillars representing gigantic serpents and sculptured standard bearers frighten off the faithful who would enter the sanctuary. At the base of the temple lies the Court of a Thousand Carved Columns, some of which are square, some round, decorated with different elaborate reliefs. It is one of the feats of archaeology that this site of Maya and Toltec culture was fully brought to light within seventeen years after the excavations had been undertaken in 1925.

44

30   Progreso, the main port of Yucatan. The ship is being loaded with sisal hemp which is made of the agave, called maguey by the Mexicans. It is being supplanted by synthetic fibers.

31   Woman from Oaxaca selling serapes. She belongs to the Zapotec tribe.

32   Monte Albán. A big urn made of black clay stands in a niche in the façade. It represents the corn god. See text, p. 19.

33   Monte Albán. Since 1931, archaeologists have excavated temples and tombs on this mountain plateau. See text, p. 17.

34   Monte Albán. Next to a temple situated on the western part of the plateau one suddenly comes upon strange reliefs carved on stone slabs. The limbs of these religious figures are strangely twisted and glyphs pour from their mouths. See text, p. 18.

35   Virgin Forest in the Quintana Roo territory near the Guatemalan border. Huts inhabited by Mayas. See text, p. 16.

36   The Yagul ruins are located between Mitla and Oaxaca. There are two vast excavation sites: a kind of Acropolis and dwellings built about the same time as Mitla, i. e. 1000 A.D.

37   Market day in Tlacolula. Tastefully arranged flower bouquets await buyers. People meet and exchange goods and news. See text, p. 20.

38   Market day in Tlacolula. Every Mexican dish contains either sweet or hot chilis. Fourteen types of chilis, in a variety of colors and pungency, are offered on hand-woven mats. See text, p. 20.

39   Market day in Tlacolula. There isn't a market without its herb woman. She labels the bags with the names of the diseases which can be healed with her herbs. The one on the upper left-hand side is against impotence, the one next to it is for women's complaints, while its neighbor is an infusion for liver ailments. There are also herbs against bronchitis, varicose veins, biliousness and pulmonary afflictions. See text, p. 20.

40   A Zapotec Indian praying in the 14th-century church in Tlacolula. His wife's head and body are covered by a *rebozo,* a big shawl frequently worn by Mexican women who also wrap them around their heads, turban-style. See text, p. 22.

41   The decorations on the sacred buildings in Mitla consist of thousands of small, carefully cut stone plates and mosaics which form recurrent patterns. Patio of the Hall of the Columns. The ancestors of these three Zapotec women lived near these buildings. Their government was theocratic (1000–1400 A.D.).

42   Palace in Mitla, near Oaxaca, a Zapotec sanctuary from 1000–1400 A.D. After the Conquest, the Spaniards built a church dedicated to "the new God" in the midst of the sacred buildings.

43   Flowering tree in the Taxco region in the state of Guerrero.

44   Old Zapotec near Mitla.

45   Farmers who brew the popular alcoholic drink known as pulque are called *tlachiqueros*. See text, p. 23.

46   It takes several years for the maguey (agave) to bloom. See text, p. 23.

47   This god of pulque stands in the patio of the National Museum of Anthropology in Mexico City. The figure which is an Huastec sculpture showing Toltec influence, originally came from Tihuatlán, state of Veracruz. As a sign of his divinity he carries a hare, the symbol of the god of pulque; it signifies drunkenness. His foam beard is typical (1100–1400 A.D.).

48   Mornings and evenings the *tlachiquero* sucks the *agua miel*, the honey water, from the maguey by means of a gourd perforated at both ends. See text, p. 23.

49   A donkey carries the *agua miel* to the hacienda by itself and also returns on its own.

50   In the evening, the *tlaquicheros* meet in front of the hacienda to sing a thanksgiving hymn to the Virgin. See text, p. 23.

51   The Xochicalco sanctuary, south of Cuernavaca. Much remains unknown about it. It shows the influence of both the Mayas and the Toltecs. The symbolism of the reliefs seems to have mattered to the builders more than anything else. Plumed serpents coil and uncoil. Between them there are warriors and calendar dates. The relief is sharply outlined and finely cut. Originally everything was brightly colored.

52   National Museum of Anthropology. This classical Maya relief (600 A.D.) is on exhibit in the Maya Hall; it is the right-hand panel of a triptych. It comes from Jonuta, state of Tabasco. The kneeling figure seems to be praying. The glyphs in the upper left-hand corner stand for blossoms.

53   The largest monolith in the country was taken to Mexico City from the village of Coatlinchán near Texcoco and was set up in front of the National Museum of Anthropology. It is an artifact of the Teotihuacán civilization and represents the rain god. See text, p. 24.

54   National Museum of Anthropology. This unique rectangular roof measuring 5400 square yards covers part of the patio. Under it, plants grow in still waters. See text, p. 24.

55   National Museum of Anthropology. The monolithic Aztec calendar stone, a disc 12 feet in diameter, weighs twenty-four tons. It used to be near the Cathedral, in front of the small Temple of the Sun, in Tenochtitlán which nowadays is part of Mexico City. It was used for worship of the sun, then considered to be the most powerful god. The stone indicates four prehistoric periods of the universe and the twenty days into which the month of the Aztec calendar was divided. Day in, day out, Mexican children are brought here to learn about their ancestors. The desire to teach makes itself felt throughout the Museum.

56   National Museum of Anthropology. Large clay vessel, a *brasero*, found on the Gulf Coast. The Aztec god Tlaloc – earrings with snakes, ornamental rings around the eyes, mouth mask with teeth. 15th century A.D.

57   National Museum of Anthropology. Coatlicue. Of Aztec origin. It represents Mother Earth who is the mother of all 400 Aztec gods. Her skirt is made of snakes, the buckle of her girdle is a human head, the necklace consists of hands and hearts, and her head is formed by two snakes hissing at each other.

58   The Nevado de Toluca volcano. Giant pine trees grow at an altitude of 12,675 feet. Cornfields in the foreground.

59   Malinalco. The pedestal of this Aztec temple resembles a pyramid with a flight of stairs leading to the temple entrance. See text, p. 24.

60   Pottery market in Toluca. Two Indian women examine the crockery.

61   The church of Santa Maria Tlancualpicán, state of Morelos.

62   San Prisca in Taxco. This is a silver mining region. A Mexican by the name of Borda, who made his fortune there, donated this extraordinary church designed by the architects Diego Durán and Juan Caballero. It was built in 1758. On the façade of rose-colored stone one can see Santa Prisca and San Sebastián. The two upper stories of the twin towers (height 156 feet) are elaborately baroque. The dome is covered with tiles brought from Puebla and from Talavera in Spain. The inside of the church is in the exuberant Churrigueresque style.

63   On January 17th, the Feast of St. Anthony the Abbot, children bring their pets to the Blessing of the Animals.

64   Bridge on the way to Acapulco built during the colonial period. Tropical forest.

65   Indian woman from Guerrero grinding corn on the *malcachete* which has been in use for 2000 years. It consists of a slightly hollow stone slab and a stone roller.

66   A beach at Acapulco. The girl carries *calebazas*, one of many varieties of pumpkins. See text, p. 26.

67   Acapulco. Far from the bathing crowd, fishermen go out in their boats to the Pacific Ocean. Their catch supplies numerous hotels in Acapulco.

68   Acapulco. Evening on one of the bays.

69   Acapulco. Sunset.

70   Fiesta in Cuetzalán. The men wear white trousers and white shirts. See text, p. 27.

71   Fiesta in Cuetzalán. The most amazing spectacle is their headgear. See text, p. 27.

72   Fiesta in Cuetzalán. The most beautiful spectacle are the dances performed by the "cuetzalines." See text, p. 27.

73   Fiesta in Cuetzalán. San Andres, the patron saint of the neighboring village, is carried into the church. See text, p. 27.

74   Puebla. The Cathedral, a huge building both sturdy and compact, rises near the main square, the *zócalo*. See text, p. 28.

75   Puebla. View of the Chapel of the Rosary in the Church of Santo Domingo. See text, p. 29.

76   The Palafox Library dates back to the year 1646. Fifty thousand volumes representing the sum of knowledge of that time are at the reader's disposal. See text, p. 28.

77   Puebla. What a crowd! All of the boys want to sell the local paper. It is printed in a house dating back to colonial times which bears its coat of arms with pride.

78   The Vista Hermosa hacienda, an old sugar-cane farm now transformed into a luxury hotel. View of the swimming pool, the old aqueduct and the former private chapel built in the 16th century.

79   Patio of a 19th-century patrician house in Mérida, Yucatan.

80   Mexicans have always liked to masquerade. Masks serve to protect, to exalt, to hide and to frighten. Folkloric carnival masks seen in the village of Amecameca.

81   Carnival in Huejotzingo. A robber's mask.

82   Harvest festival of S. Isidro Labrador in Metepéc near Toluca. Shepherd wearing an animal mask.

83   Harvest festival of S. Isidro Labrador. Witch's mask.

84   On a clear day one can see the snow-clad volcano from the capital. Popocatepetl rises some 17,800 feet above sea level. Up to an elevation of 13,000 feet, the path leading to the crater passes through pine trees and lupine underbrush, mountain meadows and pastures. From there it climbs through boulders and lava to the snow line and the crater lake.

85   Ixtaccihuatl, 17,342 feet above sea level, is the third highest mountain in Mexico. It is crowned by eternal snows. One can go up quite far on a highway. The highest mountain in Mexico is the Pico de Orizaba or Citlaltepetl (18,696 ft). The mountain pass between Popocatepetl and Ixtaccihuatl is called the Paso de Cortés because the conqueror and his soldiers crossed it in order to reach the high valley of what is now Mexico City.

86   Ceiling above the entrance of the Church of Santo Domingo in Oaxaca. In the middle of the 17th century, the Dominicans decorated it with this delightful representation of the Tree of Jesse, the family tree of the Virgin Mary. In 1862, the desecrated building served as a stable for soldiers' horses. The interior, which had been completely destroyed, was restored after 1938. Today Santo Domingo shines again in all its gilded and multicolored splendor.

87   The small village church of San Jerónimo is situated in Tlacochahuaya, between Mitla and Oaxaca. In the 16th century Arrue covered its walls with primitive and appealing folk art. This picture represents the archangel Michael.

88   The so-called "open chapel" in Tlalmanalco is an example of plateresque Renaissance style showing Indian influence. It was built by the Franciscans in 1560, but was never finished because its rich ornaments were not in keeping with Franciscan sobriety.

89   Good Friday procession in Calpan in the state of Puebla. Each year the drama of the Crucifixion is fervently observed in all Mexican villages. The faces of the Indians reflect their emotion.

90   Façade of the Hacienda S. Antonio de Acolman damaged around 1915 during the Revolution. It was built in 1581. Today it houses an orphanage founded and directed by an American priest, Father Wasson.

91   The columns in the inner courtyard of the Hacienda S. Antonio de Acolman bear witness to the grand design of Spanish colonial estates.

92   Santa Mónica Church in Guadalajara was built at the beginning of the 18th century. The façade is in the most elaborate Churrigueresque style; even the two Columns of Solomon are completely covered with carvings.

93   Marimba players. Sunday morning in Taxco. This wooden instrument which resembles the xylophone is played simultaneously by four men. Originally it came from Yucatan.

94   Corn and beans are the staples of Mexico. To make *tortillas* kernels of corn are cooked in lime and water, ground into a dough and then shaped into small balls. Each of these balls is thrown from one hand to the other until it becomes flat and round, and finally it is baked on a heated iron plate or stone.

95   The powerful Baroque cathedral and well-kept *zócalo* in San Luís Potosí, the capital of the state of the same name. The cathedral was completed in 1737. The small, lantern-like bell tower in the center is particularly picturesque.

96   Church and Convent of San Augustín in Querétaro, built in the Baroque style in the 18th century.

97   View of Guanajuato from the mountain. This town, which lies northeast of Mexico City, is one of the most beautifully preserved examples of the old colonial style. The cathedral is situated in the center of the town. Rich silver mines abound in the surrounding mountains.

98   Coconut palms.

99   Indian lovers on a ferry crossing the Usamacinta river in the state of Tabasco.

100   Minatitlan, state of Veracruz. View of one of the large oil refineries operated by Pemex, a state-owned company.

101   Flight into Egypt. Procession figures in San Andrés Church, state of Hidalgo. Rococo, delicate and charming. 17th century.

102   Churchyard in Ixtapán de la Sal. Paper decoration on a tomb.

103   Western façade of the church in Tepotzotlán, now the National Museum. See text, p. 30.

104   Original wooden sculpture from Hueyapan, 18th century. It represents Christ falling under the weight of the Cross. National Museum, Tepotzotlán. See text, p. 32.

105   Gilded main altar in the church in Tepotzotlán. See text, p. 31.

106   The snow-covered volcano, Ixtaccihuatl, rises 17,342 feet above sea level. This Spanish colonial chapel is situated in the Amecameca valley.

107   Otomí basket weaver in the Mexquí valley.

108   Fishing boat in the harbor of Veracruz. Fishing is an important Mexican industry. About three quarters of the catch are exported to the United States. Veracruz is the most important freight and passenger harbor along the tropical Gulf coast.

109   Remnants of the Tecolapan bridge in the state of Veracruz.

110   Entire families of Otomí Indians study the alphabet together.

111   Elementary school in the Mexquí valley, a particularly poor region north of Mexico City. About 300,000 Otomí Indians live there. Children studying Spanish.

112   Cathedral of Cuernavaca. Hernando Cortés ordered that it be built in 1529, i. e. about eight years after the Conquest. The Franciscans had it built in their very own style: fortress-like, few ornaments and a low cupola. It is surrounded by a large, walled square. The photograph was taken from the roof of the Church of the Third Order of St. Francis.

113   View of the highway from Mexico City to Cuernavaca. In the background the volcanoes: to the right, Popocatepetl, to the left, Ixtaccihuatl, the broader mountain with several peaks. First the road, from which one has fine views of the capital, goes up into the mountains to a pass at an altitude of more than 9,800 feet. Then it goes down to Cuernavaca (altitude 4,500 feet) which is considered to be the "riviera" of the capital because of its subtropical climate and its wealth of flowers.

114   Reservoir near Nexaca, a large power plant in the state of Hidalgo.

115   View of the summit of Popocatepetl.

116   The Mexico City Cathedral is an imposing and powerful structure. It was built to be the church of the conquerors in the course of two and a half centuries. It is an archiepiscopal mother-church, the largest on the whole continent. See text, p. 32.

117   The new residential section of Tlaltelolco in Mexico City was planned for 60,000 inhabitants. Youngsters playing in front of their school.

118   Each year, on the 25th of July, the Indians celebrate the feast of St. James on the north side of St. James' Church in Tlaltelolco, the new residential section of Mexico City. They dance and make music in the traditional manner.

119   On All Saints' Day the Indian women keep watch near the graves of their dead. Towards morning they eat the food they have brought as an offering to them. This photograph was taken in the Mexquic Cemetery, near the capital.

120   All Saints' Day. A grocery store in Mexico City sells skulls inscribed with first names which are given away as presents.

121   All Saints' Day. On that day everyone buys the traditional *pan de muerto* (bread of the dead) and the bakers decorate their shopwindows with skeletons.

122   Indians dancing outside St. James' Chruch in Tlaltelolco in Mexico City. See text, p. 35.

123   Tlaltelolco in Mexico City. Five excavated layers have yielded destroyed pyramids, temple remains, ruined palaces and sunken graveyards. The Aztec skeletons which were discovered on this site were cleaned meticulously and will henceforward be kept under glass on the very spot where they were found.

124   Bull fight in Mexico City. El Cordobés.

125–128   *Charreada.* Although there were no horses in Mexico before the Conquest, the Mexicans became great horse lovers. *Charreadas* in which non-professional horsemen show their prowess take place in various arenas every Sunday. Skilfully they catch young bulls and fillies with their lassoes. Folk music is played and folk dances are performed.

129   Mexican girl wearing the *charro* riding costume.

130–131   The flea market – *lagunilla* – which is held every Sunday behind the *Palacio de Bellas Artes* in Mexico City offers exciting, almost surrealist, experiences to the visitor.

132   The Plaza S. Domingo is one of the oldest squares in Mexico City. The Spanish Viceroys ordered the building of the arcades. The Inquisition held its meetings in these buildings which were occupied later by the Faculty of Medicine. Under the arcades, public scribes sit behind their typewriters. For a small fee they prepare love letters as well as income tax returns for the illiterate.

133   Indian couple with child.

134   Sunday afternoon in Xochimilco. A network of canals surrounds many islands on which florists plant their gardens. It is the last remnant of the Texcoco Lake which covered all of the high valley of Mexico at the time of the Aztecs. Poplars and willows abound. Particularly on Sundays it is a favorite excursion spot for the inhabitants of Mexico City and many tourists. All the boats are bedecked with flower garlands; some of them carry mariachi bands. Serapes and refreshments are offered for sale from boat to boat as they glide among the green waterplants which float on the canals. Indian women catch up to the gondolas in their dugouts and smilingly offer white and red lilies, violets and carnations. Marimba bands play in the restaurants along the shore. The whole scene is loud and colorful.

135   The Azteca football stadium in Mexico City, inaugurated in 1966, seats 105,000 people. Those who purchase expensive tickets can drive right up to the loges in their cars.

136   Competitors in the pre-Olympic tryouts dive from the tower of the swimming stadium of the Polytechnic High School in Mexico City.

137   Swimming stadium of the Polytechnic High School in Mexico City. Pre-Olympic competition.

138   Otomí children.

139   Mexico City is the highest city in the world with more than one million inhabitants (altitude 7,350 ft.). View from the Hilton Hotel on the crossroads of the Avenida Insurgentes and the Paseo de la Reforma.

140   For the sake of tradition the old building which houses the *Museo Nacional de Artes e Industrias Populares* has been allowed to stand on the Avenida Juarez between the Hotel Alameda and some modern office buildings.

141   The *Museo de Arte Moderno* in Mexico City was opened in 1964. Works of sculpture are exhibited in the park which surrounds it. Light falls on the paintings through the huge glass walls of the museum.

142   View of the stately Paseo de la Reforma. Both skyscrapers show the influence of the Mexican architect Villagrans. In spite of its North American forerunners, modern Mexican architecture has developed its own style.

143–146   Works of art from the private collection of Dr. Kurt Stavenhagen, **Mexico City**.

143   Noble stylized mask from Teotihuacán. 300 A.D.

144   Figure from Veracruz. 600 A.D.

145   Clay figurine representing a Totonac ball player from Veracruz. About 600 A.D. The yoke around his body is decorated with a jaguar's head. Protective plates cover his knees and eyes.

146   Dog begrudging a bone to another dog. Naturalistic Colima style. Fattened dogs were considered a delicacy.

147   Siren fountain in the courtyard of the Museum of the City of Mexico.

148   Folkloric ballet in Mexico City. This group goes on a world tour every year. It is famous for the encouragement it has given to folk dancing. Shown here is the *Jarabe Tapatío,* a dance which comes from the state of Jalisco.

149   Guadalupe. This large church, which looks down upon a fenced-in square, is the shrine of the Virgin of Guadalupe, the patroness of Mexico and of all of Latin America. Enormous crowds gather here each year on December 12th, the anniversary of her apparition. Pilgrims come from all over Mexico and often cover the last mile on their knees. See text, p. 36.

150   An Indian woman, exhausted by her pilgrimage, sleeps propped against a pillar in the Guadalupe basilica.

151   The Teatro Insurgentes in Mexico City was designed by Alejandro Prieto. The façade is curved. Glass mosaics by Diego Rivera represent the history of the Mexican theatre.

152   Central section of a mural by Diego Rivera. This large mural (59 ft. by 13 ft.) adorns the hall of the Hotel del Prado in Mexico City. Diego Rivera was born in Guanajuato in 1886 and died in Mexico City in 1957. He achieved world-wide recognition during his lifetime. From 1921 on, the subjects of his paintings were political and revolutionary. He said "Art is propaganda or it is not art." The partial view of the mural shown here also represents dictatorship and revolution. The work is entitled "Dream on a Sunday afternoon in the Alameda." It shows the painter as a boy with a skeleton walking by his side and, next to it, his friend and teacher Posada; behind him on the right, Rivera's wife Frieda Kahlo, and on the left, Duque Job raising his hat; in the foreground, on the left, Rivera's two daughters. Rivera painted many murals representing the liberation of the Mexican people in so simple a manner that every Indian can understand them.

153   This white chapel, which stands on a hillock near the settlement of Lomas de Cuernavaca, is visible from far away. It was built by an ingenious engineer, by the name of Candela. His boldly designed concrete roofs cover a number of chuchers, markets, hotels and garages. Usually they are either undulated or dome-shaped and very pleasing to the eye.

154   The Mexican painter David Alfaro Siqueiros.

155   A few years ago, the Administration of Mexico City opened a *Centro medico*, a medical center open to everyone and provided it with the most modern equipment. This mural painted by Siqueiros can be seen in the lobby of the cancer hospital.

156   View of the world-famous University of Mexico City, which was built on a lava field. In the foreground, mural high relief by Siqueiros, representing the progress of the sciences. Behind it, the building housing the offices of the president of the university. On the right, the main library. Juan O'Gorman is the architect who designed its mosaic walls which represent Mexican culture before and after the colonial period. Two million books are kept in it; the lighting is artificial to protect them from the bright sun.

157   Five colored stone towers mark the site of a satellite town outside Mexico City. The idea was conceived by Mathias Göritz, a German sculptor.

158   Chapultepec Park. There are men with clouds of colorful balloons everywhere. Today there is a large crowd. See text, p. 38.

159 Chapultepec Park. On Sunday mornings young men are taught tailoring here.

160 Chapultepec Park. A woman teaches young girls and housewives to prepare sauces with variations. An aroma of thyme and onions hangs in the air.

161–162 Chapultepec Park. Courses in mathematics, basic electrical engineering, languages – even in Esperanto – are given here.

163 Chapultepec Park. Practical advice on beauty culture is given to women and young girls.

164 Chapultepec Park. Sign posts indicating the various subjects of instruction are propped against enormous old ahuehuete trees.

165 Mexico is a young nation.

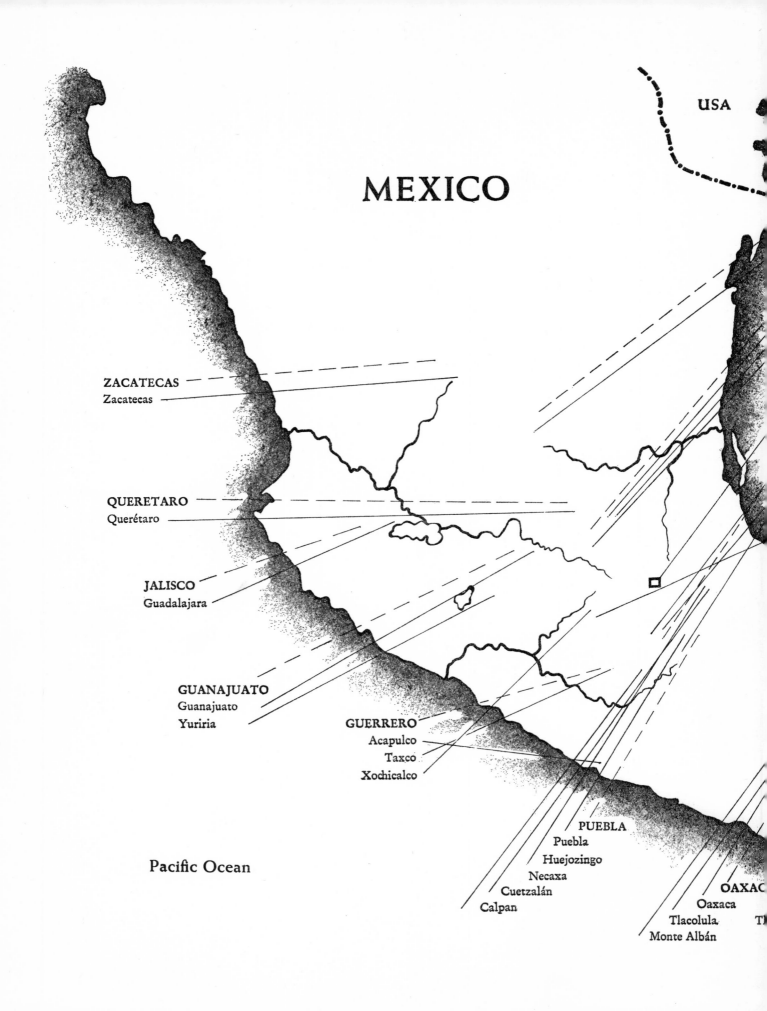

MEXICO

USA

ZACATECAS
Zacatecas

QUERETARO
Querétaro

JALISCO
Guadalajara

GUANAJUATO
Guanajuato
Yuriria

GUERRERO
Acapulco
Taxco
Xochicalco

Pacific Ocean

PUEBLA
Puebla
Huejozingo
Necaxa
Cuetzalán
Calpan

OAXAC
Oaxaca
Tlacolula
Monte Albán

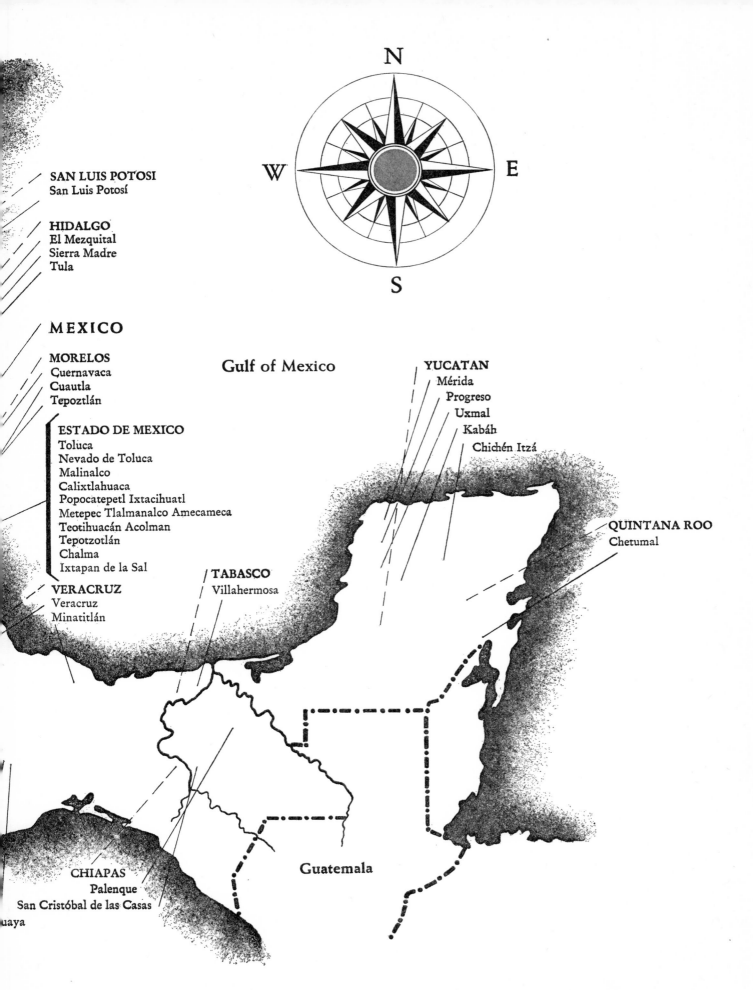

SAN LUIS POTOSI
San Luis Potosí

HIDALGO
El Mezquital
Sierra Madre
Tula

MEXICO

MORELOS
Cuernavaca
Cuautla
Tepoztlán

ESTADO DE MEXICO
Toluca
Nevado de Toluca
Malinalco
Calixtlahuaca
Popocatepetl Ixtacihuatl
Metepec Tlalmanalco Amecameca
Teotihuacán Acolman
Tepotzotlán
Chalma
Ixtapan de la Sal

VERACRUZ
Veracruz
Minatitlán

TABASCO
Villahermosa

Gulf of Mexico

YUCATAN
Mérida
Progreso
Uxmal
Kabáh
Chichén Itzá

QUINTANA ROO
Chetumal

CHIAPAS
Palenque
San Cristóbal de las Casas

Guatemala

uaya

Explanations for the photographs which follow begin on page 41.

6

8

7

9

11 → 12   13

17

1

2

MUSEO NACIONAL

54

53   55

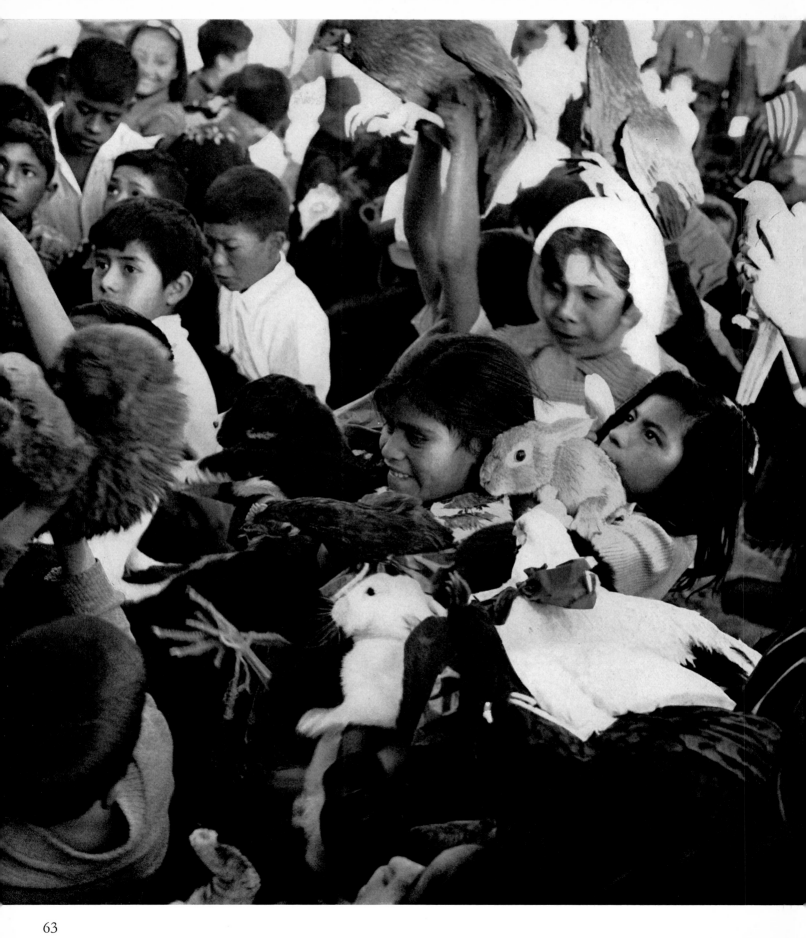

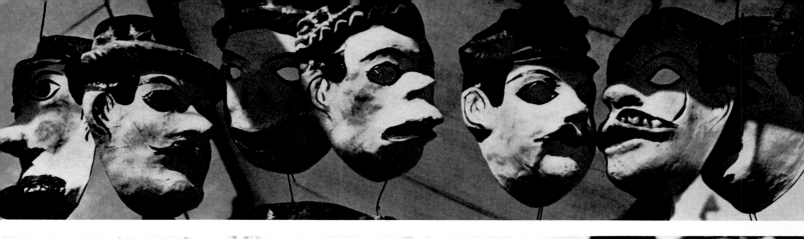

1

111

127

128

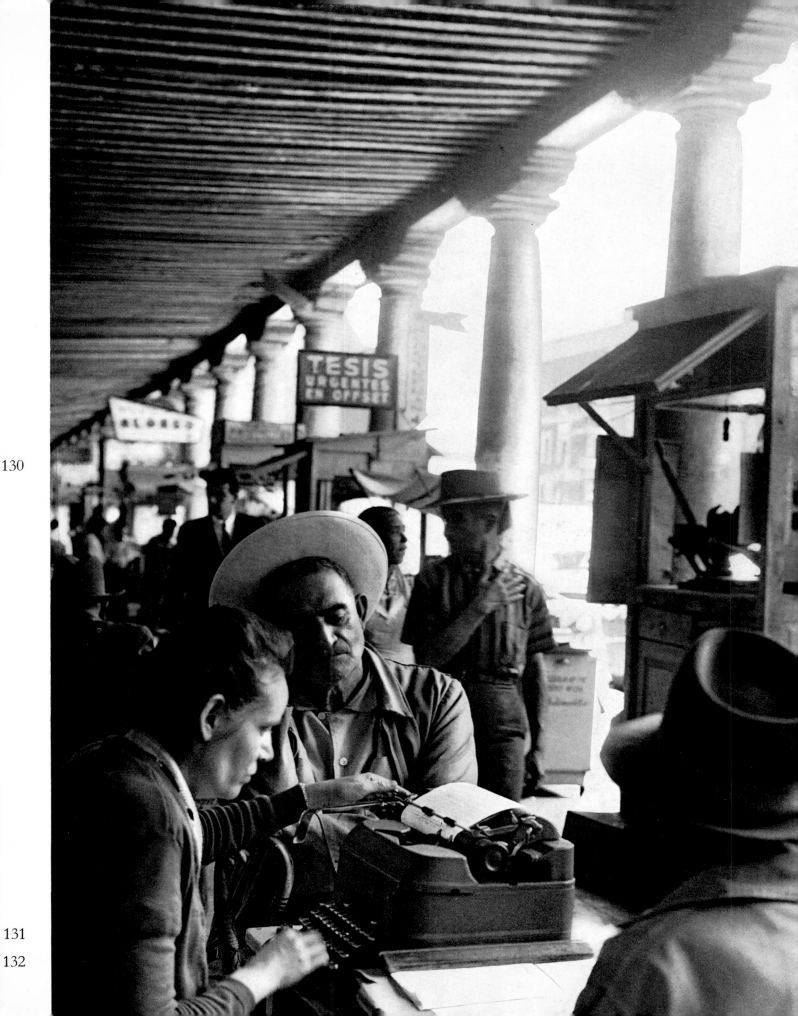

136

144

155

160—164   →165